Shrimad Bhagavad Gita

Shri Vande Bharti

Table of Contents

DEDICATION

I dedicate this interpretation to all those who seek the eternal truth.

Introduction

When all efforts of preventing a war between cousins Kauravas and Pandavas failed, both sides confronted each other on the battlefield of Kurukshetra for the epic war of Mahabharata - a war that was a result of Kauravas' jealousy and greed for power and wealth - they had swindled the kingdom from their cousins, Pandavas, in a game of dice and humiliated them by trying to disrobe their wife Draupadi, finally exiling them from the kingdom for 13 years.

It is on this battlefield that the Supreme, through his Avatar Shri Krishna, imparted this profound knowledge to Arjun - through his knowledge the Supreme restored Arjun's equilibrium which was addled by emotions and mundane conflicts - who refused to fight his kith and kin.

Every person's mind is riddled with emotions and mundane conflicts, irrespective of the circumstances, time, and place - the profound knowledge imparted by the Supreme is eternal, it transcends the boundaries of time and place.

It holds the answers to the questions that mankind has been asking since the dawn of time, questions like what is the purpose of this life? What is a person's highest duty? How can one act fairly in every situation? What happens when this life ends? Why is their misery in this world? Why are my prayers not being answered? Is there a God? If so, where is he? Why can't we see him?

If you have similar questions, then stick around to find out - this concise edition of Shrimad Bhagavad Gita has all the answers, it is a quick read and without any commentary, the knowledge within Gita is profound yet simple enough to understand without the need for commentary.

If however you have any questions about Shrimad Bhagavad Gita, then feel free to email them to me on GitaKiVaani@gmail.com.

1. Arjun's Desolation

Dhritrashtra:

O Sanjay, after gathering on the holy field of Kurukshetra with the desire to fight, what did my sons and the sons of Pandu do?

Sanjay:

On observing the Pandava army standing in military formation, King Duryodhan approached his teacher Dronacharya, and spoke the following words.

Respected teacher! Behold the mighty army of Pandu's sons, so expertly arrayed for battle by your own gifted disciple, the son of Drupad. Behold in their ranks are many powerful archers, like Bheem, Arjun, Yuyudhan, Virat, and Drupad who are all Maharathi.

There are also accomplished heroes like Dhrishtaketu, Chekitan, the gallant King of Kashi, Purujit, Kuntibhoj, and Shaibya who is strong as a bull amongst men. In their ranks, they also have the courageous Yudhamanyu, the gallant Uttamauja, the son of Subhadra, and the sons of Draupadi, who are all great warriors.

O the best of Reincarnates, hear too about the principal generals on our side, who are especially qualified to lead. These I now recount unto you. There are personalities like yourself, Bheeshma, Karna, Kripa, Ashwatthama, Vikarn, and Saumdatta's son [Bhurishrava], who are ever victorious in battle.

Also, there are many other heroic warriors, who are prepared to lay down their lives for my sake. They are all skilled in the art of warfare, and equipped with various kinds of weapons. The strength of our army is unlimited and we are safely marshaled by Grandsire Bheeshma, while the strength of the Pandava army, carefully marshaled by Bheem, is limited.

Therefore, I call upon all the generals of the Kaurava army now to give full support to Grandsire Bheeshma, even as you defend your respective strategic points.

Then, the grand old man of the Kuru dynasty, the glorious patriarch Bheeshma, blew his conch shell like a lion's roar, bringing joy to Duryodhan. Thereafter, conches, kettledrums, bugles, trumpets, and horns suddenly blared forth, and their combined sound was overwhelming.

Then, from amidst the Pandava army, seated in a glorious chariot drawn by white horses, Madhav and Arjun blew their Divine conch shells. Hrishikesh blew his conch shell, called Panchajanya, and Arjun blew the Devadutta. Bheem, the voracious eater and performer of herculean tasks, blew his mighty conch, called Paundra.

King Yudhishthir blew the Anantavijay, while Nakul and Sahadev blew the Sughosh and Manipushpak respectively. The excellent archer and king of Kashi, the great warrior Shikhandi, Dhrishtadyumna, Virat, and the invincible Satyaki, Drupad, the five sons of Draupadi, and the mighty-armed Abhimanyu, son of Subhadra, all blew their respective conch shells, O Ruler of the earth.

The terrific sound thundered across the sky and the earth, and shattered the hearts of your sons, O Dhritarasthra.

Then, the son of Pandu, Arjun, who had the insignia of Hanuman on the flag of his chariot, took up his bow. Seeing your sons arrayed against him, O King, Arjun requests Shri Krishna, the Infallible One, to draw their chariot in-between both armies so that he may look at the warriors arrayed for battle, whom he must fight in this great combat. He says that he desires to see those who have come here to fight on the side of your evil-minded son, wishing to please him.

O Dhritrashtra, having thus been addressed by Arjun, the conqueror of sleep; Shri Krishna then drew the magnificent chariot between the two armies. In the presence of Bheeshma, Dronacharya, and all the other kings, Shri Krishna says: O Pritha's son, behold these Kurus gathered here.

There, Arjun could see stationed in both armies, his fathers, grandfathers, teachers, maternal uncles, brothers, cousins, sons, nephews, grand-nephews, friends, fathers-in-law, and well-wishers. Seeing all his relatives present there, Arjun, the son of Kunti, was overwhelmed with compassion, and with deep sorrow, spoke the following words.

Arjun:

O Krishna, seeing my own kinsmen arrayed for battle here and intent on killing each other, my limbs are giving way and my mouth is drying up. My whole body shudders and my hair are standing on ends. My bow Gandeev is slipping from my hand and my skin is burning all over; my mind is in a quandary and whirling in confusion.

I am unable to hold myself steady any longer. O Krishna, killer of the Keshi demon, I only see omens of misfortune. I do not foresee how any good can come from killing my own kinsmen in this battle. O Krishna, I do not desire the victory, kingdom, or the happiness accruing it.

Of what avail will be a kingdom, pleasures, or even life itself, when the very persons for whom we covet them, are standing before us for battle? Teachers, fathers, sons, grandfathers, maternal uncles, grandsons, fathers-in-law, grand-nephews, brothers-in-law, and other kinsmen are present here.

O Madhusudan, Even if I get the dominion over the three worlds, let alone this Earth - I won't kill them; O Janardan, what pleasure will we derive from the sin of killing these desperados, sons of Dhritrashtra? O Madhav, how can we hope to be happy by killing Dhritrashtra's sons and our own kinsmen?

They are overtaken by greed and see no wrong in annihilating their relatives or betraying their friends; Yet O Janardan, why should we, who can clearly see the crime in killing our kindred, not turn away from this sin?

When a dynasty is destroyed, its traditions get vanquished, and the family strays from the path of religion. As a result, the family and its women are corrupted and distanced from their lineage, spawning tainted offspring. The future generations born in such a family are from corrupted wombs and know not to respect their ancestors and to whom they will offer no obeisance.

And thus the future generations of a once great dynasty will bring about their own downfall by destroying the great values which they were themselves responsible for carrying forward. O Janardan [Krishna], I have heard from the learned that those who destroy family traditions dwell in hell for eternity.

Alas! In our wisdom we see ourselves about to commit such a great sin of killing our kinsmen for a throne and luxuries it entails; I would rather have Dhritrashtra's sons find me unarmed on the battlefield and slay me.

Sanjay:

Speaking thus, Arjun puts down his bow and arrows, and falls into the seat of his chariot, his mind confused and burdened with grief.

2. Sankhya Yog

Sanjay:

Seeing Arjun overwhelmed with sorrow and his eyes full of tears, Shri Krishna spoke, offering Arjun the most precious wisdom of the universe.

Lord Shri Krishna:

Why has this dejection at this critical juncture befallen you, O Arjun? It is unworthy of a good man, heaven-excluding & infamy-bringing. Do not yield to impotence, O Pritha's son, it ill-fits you; Casting aside this faint heartiness, get up, tormentor of foes and fight.

Arjun:

How can I attack Bhishma & Drona with arrows, O Slayer of Madhu, those who are fit of my worship, O Slayer of foes? Instead of killing these honorable Souls, it's better to eat begged food on earth. Wouldn't killing these wealth-craving teachers stain our pleasures with their blood? Unclear who is the stronger, whether we'll win or they'll defeat us. Having slain whom we wouldn't care to live on, yet they are facing us, and siding with the sons of Dhritrashtra.

My warrior dharma is overcome by helplessness. I pray as your disciple, O Krishna, do teach me what my correct duty is. Because even if I attain the flourishing kingdom of earth and the lordship of the heavens, how would it remove my grief, which withers my senses.

Sanjay:

Having spoken to the Lord of senses [Krishna]; Arjun [conqueror of sleep & tormentor of foes] says, "I will not fight", O Govind, fell silent.

O Dhritrashtra, thereafter, in the midst of both armies, Lord of senses [Krishna], as if smiling, says to grief-stricken Arjun.

Lord Shri Krishna:

You grieve for those who deserve no grief and you speak like a wise Pundit, the wise grieve not over what evolves and dissolves ever. There never was a time when you, I, and all these kings never existed, nor shall they ever cease to exist hereafter.

Just as the embodied Soul continuously passes from childhood to youth to old age similarly, at the time of death, the Soul passes into another body. The wise are not deluded by this. The sensory organs feel, O Kunti's son, the cold, the heat, the pleasure, and the pain; these are ever-changing and transient, bear these feelings, 0 scion of Bharat.

O Arjun, noblest amongst men, only those who weather these temporary feelings of grief and happiness while maintaining their equilibrium can attain Moksha [liberation from the cycle of birth & death]. The Soul is eternal and never ceases to be unlike the body, which is temporary. The seers have observed this truth after studying both.

The Soul is imperishable and no one can destroy it; all the bodies in the universe are pervaded by it. Only the body, within which this indestructible Soul resides, is perishable. The Soul within is eternal, and thus, O Arjun, fight now.

He who views the Soul as the slayer & he who treats the Soul as slain are both ignorant, for the Soul neither slays nor is it slain. Soul is neither born, nor does it ever die, never having been, shall never cease to be. The Soul is unborn, it is eternal, immortal, and ageless. It is not destroyed when the body is destroyed.

He who knows this self as un-perishing, eternal, unborn, unchanging that person, O Pritha's son, how can he slay or be slain? As a person sheds worn-out garments and wears new ones, likewise, at the time of death, the Soul casts off its worn-out body & migrates to a new one.

Soul cannot be pierced with weapons, nor can be burned by fire, drowned in water, or dissipated by wind. The Soul is impenetrable, incombustible, un-drownable and indispersable; everlasting, all pervading, firm, unmoving, and ancient.

Without form, beyond comprehension, immutable is the Soul; Now you know, therefore you should not grieve. Even if you regard the Soul to constantly go through the cycle of birth & death, O mighty-armed, you shouldn't grieve. What is born will certainly die, and rebirth is certain of which dies, So you shouldn't grieve for the inevitable.

Unmanifested is the primal state of beings, manifestation is their middle state, and O scion of Bharat, unmanifested again after death, what is there then to grieve? Some regard the Soul as marvelous, others marvel to learn about it, and yet some others are unable to understand its marvels, even after hearing about it.

The dweller [Soul] is constant, unslayable, and present in everybody, O Bharat, Therefore you shouldn't mourn for anybody; as a Kshatriya [warrior], your duty is to fight for and uphold righteousness. So do not waver, O Arjun, fortunate are the Kshatriya who are afforded this opportunity. A virtuous battle that grants them passage to Heaven. But abandoning this war and rejecting your duty will incur infamy, and sin.

For a person of your repute and stature, the mark of a deserter and cowardice will be worse than death. The great warriors beside whom you have fought will despise you for abandoning a fight and those you fought against will treat you lightly. Belittling you, your honor, and truly your might, what could be more painful than that?

If killed in action ascend to Heaven or be victorious & rule this earth; Therefore arise, O Kunti's son, to fight with determination. Grief or happiness, victory or defeat, remain indifferent to the outcome and fight, thus you shall incur no sin.

Thus I've explained to you Gyana Yog, the intellectual perspective of life. Now listen, O Pritha's son, as I explain Karma Yog, with which you can remain free from the bondage of karmas. Never is this path futile or harmful even a little practice of this Dharma can save the Karmyogi from the terrible fear of death.

In this [Karmyog] there is a singular understanding of resolute determination. However, O scion of Kuru, for the ignorant, these understandings are many-branched & innumerable. In flowery speech indulge the ignorant, teaching them that the Vedas are the only and final truth. And with their Souls steeped in desire for heaven, and [flowery speech] offering rebirth as the result, they perform many ceremonies for securing wealth & power.

In their pursuit of wealth & power the hearts of such devotees are captivated. Not in the understanding of the Divine. Vedas only treat the three traits of Nature [Satva, Rajas, & Tamas], you must grow above and beyond these three traits, O Arjun, free yourself from contradictions of Happiness & Grief, Success & Failure etc. etc. forever being rooted in the Self, untroubled by acquisition & preservation, and self-controlled.

Of what use is a reservoir in a place which is flooded with water, Of same utility are the Vedas to one who is God-knowing & enlightened. In action alone is your freedom, but never in its results. Act not with a motivation for a return, neither give in to inaction.

Performing actions as per Yoga, abandoning all attachment [of the outcome], O victor of wealth, remaining equanimous in success & failure, this equanimity is called Yoga. Far inferior are actions taken for [selfish] reasons, O victor of wealth, self-defeating are the ones, who act selfishly.

Imbued with poised reason one forsakes good & ill deeds, so strive for this Yoga and become skillful in it. Having taken the path of performing selfless actions without an expectation of a reward, Sages freed themselves from the endless cycle of rebirth & attained the blissful state.

Only after crossing this mire of delusion your reason will be indifferent to heard [learnt] and to be heard [to be learned]; Your intellect will cease to be bewildered by any other preaching, for you will already have attained Yoga [enlightenment].

Arjun:

O Keshav [Krishna], what language does such an enlightened one speak? O Keshav, How does he talk, sit, walk or conduct himself?

Lord Shri Krishna:

When he forsakes cravings of all worldly desires, and is absolutely content with his own companionship - he is said to be of stable reasoning. Unperturbed in crisis or immune to elation; free from passion, fear, and anger - He is the stable sage.

Unattached in every way, in whatever he gets, whether fair or foul, Neither rejoices nor bemoans, his understanding becomes stable. Like a tortoise draws itself into its shell, who withdraws his senses from his sense organs, attains poise.

Desires recede from the mind of who abstains, so does affection, upon realizing the Truth. The senses are strong, O Kunti's son, and their pull can sway even the most intelligent and tolerant of men. Only they can keep their senses under control, who are devoted to Me, Only with disciplined senses, their reason becomes stable.

The mind dwells on objects & develops attachments, from attachments, desires are born. These desires [when unfulfilled] turn into anger. From anger arises delusion, therefrom confusion of memory, from confusion of memory, loss of reason, with reason gone, the man is lost.

By renouncing affection and aversion, senses roam free [of attachments] to objects. With mind being under one's control, man becomes conscious of his pure self and attains tranquility; with cessation of all suffering [due to detachment], tranquility is born, and with tranquility the reason soon is steadied.

There cannot be stable reasoning without control over senses, without sense control there cannot be meditation, without meditation there cannot be peace, and how can there be happiness without peace? Sensual desires can rock a person's intellect like the strong gusts of wind rock an unanchored sail boat and lead it astray.

Therefore, O Mighty Armed, who has completely withdrawn his desires from sense objects, his steadiness is established. What seems as night for all beings, the self-controlled keeps awake. In what seems like day for all beings, sleeps the sage, who sees.

As ocean remains still even when the gushing rivers steadily pour into it; Likewise desires keep flowing into whom who has attained peace, without affecting him. Who gives up desires, no longer competes for proprietorship or ego, and lives in peace.

Thus attainting this state of Brahmi [Enlightenment] O Pritha's son, he is no longer deluded. Maintaining this same state till the end [of life] attains Nirvana [Moksh].

3. Karm Yog

Arjun:

If reason [knowledge] is superior to action, O Janardan, than why do you prompt me to commit this cruel 'action', O Keshav? Contradictory statements are confusing me; let me know decisively which path is excellent.

Lord Shri Krishna:

In this world, there are two methods I have indicated before, O sinless, the Yoga of Knowledge as per Sankhyas and the Yoga of Action as per Yogis. Not by abstinence does one remain inactive. Nor by mere renunciation does he attain perfection.

Not for an instant ever can anyone rest inactive. Helplessly all are driven to action by the Tri-Gunas [three traits] of Nature. They restrain their sense organs, yet they dwell on those senses in their mind, such claimants are self-deluded hypocrites.

Those who practice self-control & regulate their senses, O Arjun, and perform their actions as per Karmyoga without coercion are superior. Perform your duteous actions. Action is superior to inaction, because if left inactive, this sojourn body will fail.

Action not performed as a Yajna [Fire-Ritual], bonds that action-doer to this world. Hence perform your actions, O Kunti's son, as a Yajna and remain bondage-free; with Yajna mankind evolved from the time of creation, The Creator, gave mankind [Yajna] as the means to prosper and propagate.

The Devas [demi-gods] you serve [through Yajna], the Devas then serve you [through rain] and you both mutually serve the all-pervading [God]. Devas [demi-gods] bestow enjoyments for performing [Yajnas], but those who do not share these enjoyments are in fact thieves.

Saints enjoy what's left-over after sharing with others & avoid sin, but those who only enjoy everything themselves are sinners. Food that sustains all beings, grows because of rains, and rains results from Yajnas - these actions are inter-dependent.

Karmas were created by Brahma and Brahma himself originated from the Almighty, that same all-pervading Almighty is forever present in the Yajna. The cycle of time keeps turning, the ones who does everything for pleasing their senses, O Pritha's son, they live in vain.

One rejoicing in the self, illumined in the self-content in the self alone, for they are free from all obligations. Neither without reason he acts or doesn't act, nor he acts for recognition. Therefore always perform all your actions selflessly, only by doing so does one attains the Supreme.

King Janak and the likes attained enlightenment by performing actions selflessly for world-harmony, and so can all others who do so. Howsoever the virtuous behave, so does the world follow, whatever standard they set, men follow unquestioningly.

There is nothing that I desire, O Pritha's son, nor anything that I cannot attain effortlessly in all Tri-Lokas [Tri-regions]. Yet, I am engaged in action [Karma]. If I were to not perform any actions [Karmas], everyone everywhere would follow suit, O Pritha's son. The worlds would perish, if I shun my actions [Karmas] the ensuing confusion would result in total annihilation of all habitants.

The ignorant act Selfishly, O Bharat, therefore the wise desiring a harmonious world, should act selflessly. Without unsettling the ignorant selfish; the wise should steadily act to educate them towards selflessness.

Depending on the Gunas, all Karmas [actions] are performed, but blinded by ego, the self thinks himself to be the doer. A knower, O mighty-armed, knows these divisions of Gunas, hence knows which action is the result of which Guna and not the 'Self'.

Those deluded, act on the basis of their Gunas and lowly acts of such dim-witted perturb themselves. Dedicate all your actions to me with a renunciated mindset, without expectation or ego; shed the fever of doubt and fight.

Whosoever practices this teaching of mine faithfully, they are undoubtedly liberated from the bondage of Karmas [actions] But those who are negligently critical and do not practice this teaching of mine remain devoid of all true knowledge, regard such ignorant folk to be doomed.

All people act based upon their Gunas [traits of nature], controlled by these Gunas, how can one restraint themselves? Senses and their desires inherently imbue passion and anger; yield not to them, they are the obstacles of the [righteous] path.

Better is one's self-duty seemingly meritless, than performing another's duty; dying in the discharge of one's duty is far better than being proselytized out of fear.

Arjun:

Then what moves a man to commit sins? Even though unwillingly, O Varshaneya [Krishna], but as if compelled.

Lord Shri Krishna:

It is the craving; it is the anger, due to Rajoguna [Rajas – one out of the three traits of Nature]; it is all-consuming, the most sinful, and the worst enemy on this earth. As fire is enveloped by smoke, or mirror by dust, fetus by membrane, so is the craving enveloped by Rajoguna.

Rajoguna is the perpetual enemy that hides knowledge from the seeker, O Kunti's son, by the insatiable fire of desire. Senses, mind, and intelligence are its stations. Through these, desires envelope knowledge & deludes the body-dweller [Soul].

So first discipline your senses, O best of Bharats, and slay this [Rajoguna] sinful destroyer of knowledge & wisdom; Senses are stronger than the body, Mind is stronger than the Senses, Intellect is stronger than the mind, however the Soul is far superior. But Rajoguna is stronger than the intellect and hence it controls the mind, slay this enemy [desire], O mighty-armed, as this foe is hard to vanquish.

4. Gyan Karm Yog

Lord Shri Krishna:

I first taught this Yoga to Viwaswat [Sun], Viwaswat taught Manu & Manu taught Ikshwaku; Thus this knowledge was passed down from generation to generation for eons by the Sage Kings, but with the passage of time it was lost to mankind, O tormentor of foes.

The same ancient Yoga, I am teaching you today, which is the most profound mystery, because you are my devotee & friend.

Arjun

You were born recently, Viwaswat [Sun] was born at creation, How could have you taught it to the Sun at the time of Creation?

Lord Shri Krishna:

Many have been my births as well yours, O Arjun, I remember all of them, but you do not, O tormentor of foes. Even though I am unborn, eternal, & Lord of all beings, I manifest my transcendental energy into this form to be discernible by mortal beings.

Whenever there is decay of Dharma, O Bharat, and growth of Adharma, I assume a body-form to protect the good and destroy the evil and to re-establish true Dharma, I have manifested again and again for eons. Whosoever comprehends the purpose of My divine birth and its true essence, they upon shedding their body [dying] is not reborn, but comes to me, O Arjun.

Freed from attachment, fear and anger, mind absorbed in Me, refuged in Me, Purified in the fire of knowledge, have many attained My Bliss. In whatever way they pray to me, I accept those who at last tread My path, O Pritha's son, whenever they may commence.

But those who desire gratification here [in this mortal realm] serve demigods. Soon they attain such gratifications.

I created the four classes based on the division of Guna Karma [Traits of Nature], I created them to be passive & immutable. Neither am I affected by Karmas, nor do I relish its rewards those who know me thus, is not bound by action. Thus the learned performed their actions to achieve liberation, you must also perform your actions similarly as they did in the past.

What is Karma [action] and what is Akarma [inaction] knowing the difference is puzzling. The difference I shall explain, knowing which will save you from inauspicious. It is necessary to know the nature of action, as well as that of forbidden action. Necessary also to know the nature of inaction, mysterious is the path of action.

He who acts when others are inactive and remains inactive when others react is wise & expert doer of actions. Whose all commencements of deeds are without self-gratification; Tempered in the fires of knowledge, he shall be known as a Pundit.

Who abandons all desire for rewards from his Karmas [actions], remains forever satiated & independent even when engaged in Karmas [actions], he accrues no Karmas. Hoping for no rewards, with a self-controlled mind, without any desires for personal possessions, using the body only for selfless acts, he remains sin free.

Content with unsought gain, without contradictions, equanimous in success or failure, though acting, he remains unbound [by Karmas] freed from all attachments, established in knowledge. When Karmas [Actions] are performed as Yajnas, all activities disintegrate into ether like oblations.

Every deed as a Yajna, every Karma [action] as an oblation, knowledge as the divine fire [of this Yajna], and Me as the presiding deity; those who perform all their Karmas [actions] this way, attain Moksha. Devas [demigods] are invoked through Yajnas for fulfilling desires, then there are those who invoke the fire-god to perform Yajnas for Yajna's sake.

Others offer their learning etc. in the fire of restraint. Others offer their voice [give-up speaking] etc. in the fire of the senses. Some offer their sensual desires and life actions in the illumined fires of knowledge by becoming a Hermit/Monk [celibate].

Some offer their wealth for helping others, by spreading knowledge and creating means for the betterment of society. There are some who practice yogic breathing techniques to control their Gunas and awaken their Kundalini.

While some fast as a means to control their desires and cleanse their body & sins. Whosoever performs some form of Yajna attains the Supreme Eternal. Not the ones who do not, O Best of Kurus. Thus are the varieties of Yajnas as uttered by Brahma, performed by different faculties, and they all grant liberation.

Superior to ingredient oblations is the oblation of knowledge, O tormentor of foes, because the entirety of actions, O Pritha's son, culminate in knowledge. Learn this [Yajna] with humility [from a teacher], by enquiry and by service. The learned & the seers of essence will instruct you in this knowledge.

Knowing this you will no longer remain deluded O Pandava; by it you will see me present in all beings. Even if you are, of all sinners, the most sinful, with this boat of knowledge you will be able to sail across the sea of sins. As the fuel is burnt by the fire, O Arjun, similarly Karmas [actions] are burnt away in the fire of knowledge.

There is no other purer knowledge for achieving perfection in Yoga as the one that is achieved, in due time, from within. As faithful discipline their senses, they speedily gain knowledge, with knowledge gained, they easily attain supreme peace. The ignorant, devoid of faith and torn with self-doubt, perish. There is no happiness for them, neither in this world nor the next.

Who has renounced [selfish actions] Karmas like a Sanyasi [ascetic] and torn asunder the veil of doubt, such self-controlled is not bonded by Karmas [actions], O winner of wealth. Hence the doubt born & residing in your heart must be slain with this knowledge of the Self, slay that doubt, remain steady in Yoga, and rise up O Bharat.

5. Karm Sanyaas Yog

Arjun:

You have praised both Sanyas [renunciation], O Krishna, as well as the path of Karma [selfless actions] Of the two, which one is better, tell me decisively.

Lord Shri Krishna:

Sanyas [Renunciation] & Karma Yoga [Yoga of Action] both lead to the highest good. But of the two, Karma Yoga is indeed better than Sanyas. Know him to be a Sannyasi, who neither dislikes nor craves, free from contradictions, O mighty armed, such a one is easily released from bondage.

Sankhya & [Karma] Yoga being different is talked by the immature, not by the learned; one fully devoted to either path reaps the same fruit. Stature gained by Sankhyas [Sanyasis], the same is gained by the Yogis [Karma Yogis] Sankhya & Yoga are the same, only those who realize this fact, know the truth.

Attainment of Sanyas [Renunciation], O mighty armed, is harder for the untrained While a [Karma] Yogi sage reaches the Supreme earlier [than Sanyasis]. An Enriched [Karma] Yogi, Purified Soul, Victorious Soul, Conqueror of Senses; viewing all embodied as the primeval spirit, his actions remain untainted.

A [Sanyasi] considers himself being actionless, even though he sees, hears, touches, smells, eats, moves, sleeps, breathes, speaks, gives, receives, blinks; all these functions of the senses are considered Karmas [actions].

Dedicating Karmas [actions] to the Supreme, who acts without expecting a reward. He remains untouched by sin like a water droplet on a lotus-leaf; through body, mind, intellect and senses, Yogis act without expectation for a reward, but only for self-purification.

Enriched, renunciating expectation of any reward, he [Yogi] attains enduring peace. Those lacking [in Yoga], pursue selfish goals, are bound [to this mortal realm]. All Karmas renunciated, the mind lives happily in this nine-gated city [body], free from thinking themselves as the doers or the cause of anything.

Neither agency nor activity [of Karmas] is created by God nor the results of such Karmas, they are inherent in the nature [of the doer]. The Lord is never involved in any being's sinful or virtuous deeds; it is ignorance that envelopes wisdom, thereby deluding creatures.

Whose ignorance is destroyed by knowledge of the self, for them knowledge, like the sun illumines the Supreme; reason abiding in that [God], mind absorbed in that [God], rooted in that [God], devoted to that [God]; they leave [this mortal realm] never to return, as their sins are washed away by knowledge.

To a humble scholar, a Brahman, a cow, an elephant, a dog and a dog-eater are all considered equal. Even here in this mortal realm they gain [happiness], whose minds are equanimous because the Supreme is flawless, as are those whose knowledge is established. He neither rejoices on obtaining pleasantness nor grieves on obtaining the unpleasantness, such Yogi's reason remains steadfast and clear minded for being established in the Divine.

Whose Self is unaffected by external stimuli finds happiness within; such God unioned Self enjoys bliss unending. These enjoyments [external stimuli] are as verily wombs of pain, as they are fleetingly transient, O Kunti's son, and the knower is not swayed by them.

One who is able to withstand [external stimuli] on earth before casting off his body, and also the surges that are produced by craving & anger, he is an enriched happy man. He who is joyous within, who enjoys within, who is illumined within, that Yogi finds Moksh and merges with the Brahman.

Yogis enjoy divine communion having their sins worn away, dualities torn asunder, they are self-restrained and intent on welfare of all. Free of desire and anger, devotees, mind under control, Divine communion lies at hand to the knowers of Self.

Keeping external stimuli out, with eyes fixed amidst the eyebrows, equalizing inhalation & exhalation. Controlling the senses, mind and reason, a sage intent on liberation having renounced desire, who lives free of anger, is verily freed.

Enjoyer of all sacrifices and austerities and Lord of all the realms, and comrade of all beings, having known Me so, he [Yogi] attains peace.

6. Dhyan Yog

Lord Shri Krishna:

Those who abandon any expectation from their obligatory duties, is a Sanyasi as well as a Yogi, not the one who abandons Yajna or Worldly chores. That which is called Sanyas [renunciation] is also [Karma] Yoga, O Pandava, because without renunciation how can one become a Yogi?

Aspiring sages reason Karma [actions] to be the means [of achieving Yoga]; Those established in Yoga, reason tranquility [meditation] to be the means [of achieving Yoga]. But only when neither Karma nor meditation is for sensual pleasures or for rewards; does one establish himself in Yoga.

Elevate yourself in your own eyes, do not let your self-esteem fall; verily you are your own best friend & your own worst enemy. He is a friend of himself when one can control himself; Uncontrollable self becomes a hostile enemy.

A self-controlled [person] dedicated to God becomes serene & equipoised; in summer or winter, joy or sorrow, fame or infamy. Satiated with knowledge & self-realization, unperturbed and self-controlled; Yukt [enriched] is such Yogi called, to him clay, stone, or gold are all worth the same.

Who adopts the same attitude towards well-wishers, friends, foes, neutrals, and arbiters, the jealous and relatives. Even towards the pious & the sinners, he is better still. A Yogi should meditate regularly, concentrating while seated in a quiet place. Alone, with mind self-controlled, without expectation and [sense of] possession.

[Meditate] In a pure [clean] spot having prepared a firm seat, neither too high nor too low with Kusa grass, deer-skin and cloth. Concentrating & keeping in check the activities of the senses & the mind, sitting on his seat he [aspirant Yogi] should practice Yoga [meditate] for self-purity.

Holding the body, head & neck, unmoved & straight; Gazing at tip of the nose without glancing elsewhere, remain serene, fearless, and continent; Concentrating & meditating [my name] and devoted to Me.

With regular meditations a Yogi's mind is disciplined; Serene and unattached, [the Yogi] finds communion with my Divine Bliss. Yoga is not for the over-eater, nor the under-eater, nor for one who over-sleeps or under-sleeps, O Arjun. Equilibrium in eating & recreation, working, sleeping, & waking; such Yogi's sorrows are destroyed.

When the disciplined mind abides solely in the self, he is freed from yearning in all objects of desire, is then known as "Yukt" [Enriched]. As a lamp remains flicker-free in a windless place, as does the thoughts of a disciplined Yogi never wander.

When the inner joy is found [with meditation] and the mind becomes restrained through Yoga; then the Self realizes the Soul and remains satisfied. Thus the utmost happiness is found by transcending beyond senses; upon realization, he [Yogi] never forgets the Eternal Truth.

Having gained that [Self Realization], no other gain seems greater; established therein [in Self Realization] not any overwhelming sorrow can perturb the Yogi. Understand that the state of severing ties with unhappiness is known as Yoga; therefore it [Yoga] should be practiced with relentless determination.

Resolutely and completely forsaking every desire born in the mind; And with every sense organ restrained, slowly, steadily, and patiently he [Yogi's] should guide his intellect to stop worrying mindlessly. Whenever the restless & unsteady mind wanders into worrying, the Yogi should practice to bring the mind back under Self's control.

Peaceful and calmed mind grants greatest happiness to the Yogi; with such calmness comes sin-free God Realization. Thus the trained mind of a Yogi always remains sin-free; easily connects with Divinity & attains highest bliss.

Every living being's Soul is a part of the same primeval Soul that lies within himself; hence the Yoga enriched Soul considers every living being the same. Therefore who sees Me in every living being and every living being in Me, I am always visible to him & as he is to me.

Whoever realizes the oneness of everything & worships Me, as being present in each & every living being, no matter what he does - such a Yogi is always with and present in me. When one begins to realize, every other living being's happiness or sorrow as his own, O Arjun, that Yogi then becomes the greatest.

Arjun:

The Yoga of Equanimity described by you, O Madhusoodna, I do not see an enduring continuance of it due to the restlessness of the mind. The restless mind, O Krishna, is impetuous, powerful & obstinate; controlling the mind is like unsuccessfully grasping the wind.

Lord Shri Krishna:

Undoubtedly, O mighty-armed, restless mind is hard to restrain; O Kunti's son, but with practice and renunciation it can be subdued. It is difficult to control the mind for someone untrained in Yoga; But for someone who is trained [in Yoga] it is indeed possible.

Arjun:

Failed devoted aspirants, who practice Yoga, but are distracted before achieving perfection, what happens to such aspirants, O Krishna? Will the efforts of such aspirants who have wandered from either paths of Yoga, dissipate like clouds? Do such un-established aspirants, O mighty-armed, try vainly, only to lose the Eternal path?

This doubt of mine, O Krishna, only you are fit to destroy completely; none other remover of this doubt as capable as you can be found.

Lord Shri Krishna:

O Pritha's son, neither here [in the mortal realm] nor in the after world is that aspirant destroyed. My dear friend, the practitioner of auspicious [Yoga] never falls to the lower realms. The righteous aspirants reach higher realms and enjoy for long periods; then they are reborn in a pure & prosperous home or in the family of the wise Yogis the unsuccessful aspirant is reborn; but the latter is very rare in this mortal realm.

There his wisdom, from his previous birth, is rekindled; he then continues his journey towards attaining Yoga, O scion of Kuru. Pre-practiced in the previous birth, the unsuccessful aspirant is involuntarily inquisitive [about Yoga]; and this curiosity leads him to transcend the Vedic ritualism.

Striving in spirituality the Yogi is cleansed of his sins; perfected in Yoga after many rebirths, he finally reaches the ultimate destination. A Yogi is superior than an ascetic, even superior than the knower of scriptures; And certainly superior than one who acts selfishly, therefore become a Yogi, O Arjun.

And amongst the Yogis, those devoted to Me; who faithfully worship Me, I regard them the best enriched in Yoga.

7. Gyan Vighyan Yog

Lord Shri Krishna:

He whose mind is devoted to Me, O Pritha's son, depending on Me, practicing Yoga; undoubtedly merges with me, listen to know how. That knowledge & wisdom I shall impart in its entirety; knowing which, there is nothing more worthy in this world that remains to be known.

Amongst thousands of men, only a few strive for perfection in Yoga; even amongst them, very few know my true essence. Earth, water, fire, air, ether, mind, intellect, and egoism, these are the eight characteristics of nature that I created.

Apart from these lesser qualities of my primal nature; there is the life-force, O mighty-armed, which sustains this universe. These are the two wombs of all manifested living beings; they originate from Me & dissolve in Me at the end. Beyond Me there is nothing whatsoever, O victor of wealth, everything is threaded in Me, like beads on a string.

I am sapidity in water, O Kunti's son, the light in the sun & the moon; The OM [AUM] in all Vedas, sound in ether [Akash], manhood in men. The pious fragrance in earth, glow in fire; life in all beings, and austerities of the ascetics.

Know Me to be the eternal seed of every living being, O Pritha's son; I am the reason of the wise, and radiance of the illustrious. I am the strength of the strong who are devoid of selfish interests and desires; the desire in all living beings that conforms with Dharma, O best of Bharats.

And these Satvic, Rajasic, and Tamsic states of existence; Know them from Me, yet I am not in them nor they are in me. These three traits [Satva, Rajas, Tamas] delude this whole world; mesmerized by these traits, the world remains unaware of the imperishable primeval Me.

My divinity is veiled by Maya of these three traits [Satva, Rajas, Tamas] and difficult to cross; only those devoted to Me are able to get through. Un-devout to Me are the sinners, ignorant, and the vile men; Deprived of knowledge due to Maya, having demonic disposition.

Four types of pious people worship Me, O Arjun. The distressed [due to sickness or tragedy], the inquisitive, the wealth seeker, and the knowledgeable devotee, O best of Bharats. Of these 4 pious worshippers, especially the knowledgeable one is forever immersed and solely devoted to Me; to him I am dearest and he is dearest to Me.

Noble they all are [the 4 pious worshippers], but the knowledgeable should be treated as My very Self, because he is completely immersed in Me, he only seeks divine communion [Moksh]. After many rebirths, such knowledgeable [devotee] merges with Me; Realizing that it is Me [Vasudev] everywhere, such a great Soul is indeed very rare.

Those whose knowledge is enveloped by cravings, worship Demigods; Performing various rituals driven by their wants. In whichever form [a Demigod] is worshiped for receiving a reward; I steady that devotee's faith in that form.

The worshiper invokes that Demigod with his faith; whatever desires he wished for are in fact granted by Me. But those gifts are perishable, worshippers with limited understanding only reach out to Demigods, whereas my worshippers reach out to Me.

I am Indiscernible, but the unwise believe Me to be discernible; remaining ignorant of My supreme, limitless, & exalted form. Enveloped by My Yoga-Maya, I remain invisible to everybody; the deluded in this world do not know Me as the unborn & limitless.

I am aware of beings gone in the past, here in the present, O Arjun; And of those who will come in the future, but none know about Me. Torn between the contradictions of desires & aversions, O Bharat; All beings are mesmerized upon entering this mortal realm, O tormentor of foes.

Those people whose sins have been erased due to their righteous deeds; freed from the contradictions [of desires & aversions], they worship Me devotedly. They find liberation [Moksh] from aging & dying; those devoted in Me realize the Brahman through spirituality & righteous deeds. They realize that I am the Primeval Matter, Primeval Celestial, and the Primeval Yajna; Even at the time of their departure from this mortal realm, they remember the above mentioned fact about Me.

8. Akshar Brahma Yog

Arjun:

What is that Brahman, what is Adhyatma and what is Karma, O Purushottam? What is Adhibhut and Adhidaiva, why are they called so? Who and what is Adhiyajna in this body, O slayer of Madhu? At the time of departure from this mortal realm, tell me how are You remembered by the knowledgeable?

Lord Shri Krishna:

The Imperishable Supreme is Brahma. The intrinsic nature [conscience] is Adhyatma. The interaction of a being, depending upon his conscience with nature and other living beings on the whole, is Karma.

Adhibhut is the perishable union of Primeval Materials personifying the Primeval being Adhidaiva. The Adhiyajna is the primeval life-force residing in that embodied being. In the end, those who are leaving this mortal realm and had meditated on Me while living; such departing Souls, without doubt, merge with Me. Or whomsoever they meditated on while living; they will achieve them after being reincarnated, O Kunti's son.

Therefore remember Me at all times and also while fighting; surrender your mind & reason to Me, you will certainly attain Me. An un-wandering & Yoga enriched practiced intellect; dedicated to the Supreme Divine Being, O Pritha's son, comes to Me.

The All-knowing, Ancient, Sovereign, Subtler than the Subtlest, Whoever meditates upon Me; The Sustainer of all, Inconceivable form, Brighter than the Sun, beyond all Darkness; at the time of departing from this mortal realm, dedicated in devotion through Yoga's strength;

concentrating their life-force between their eye-brows, he merges with the Supreme Divine Being.

I shall describe briefly that Goal whom the Vedic scholars call the Imperishable, whom the ascetics seek by remaining celibate. Restraining all the gates of the body [Ears, Eyes, Nostrils, Mouth, Anus and Genitals], concentrating the mind in the [Chest region] heart; drawing the life-force through the forehead, in a Yogic state. Chanting the Monosyllable OM [AUM], remembering Me as the Brahman; departs from his body, he attains the Divine Path [merges with Me].

With an unswerving mind who always meditates on Me; For such Yogis it is easy, O Pritha's son, to always attain Me. Having attained Me, Yogis are freed from the cycle of rebirth and this mortal realm of sorrows; great Souls, who have achieved perfection through Yoga never suffers. Until reaching the Realm of Brahma, beings of all realms go through rebirth, O Arjun; but after reaching Me, O Kunti's Son, one is freed from rebirth.

A Day of Brahma lasts a thousand Yugas; And Brahma's Night lasts another thousand Yugas, this [period of Day & Night] is known to the wise. The unmanifested turns into manifestations at the dawn of [Brahma's] day; and merges back into the unmanifested at the dusk of [Brahma's] Night.

Multitude of beings repeatedly manifest at the dawn of Brahma's Day only to be unmanifested, O Pritha's son, helplessly at the dusk of Brahma's Night. But apart from this cycle of destructive manifestations, there is an eternal manifestation; where once manifested, one is never annihilated. That Manifest-less realm beyond Brahma is the Ultimate Path of every Yogi; Going where no one ever returns to any realm, that is My Supreme Abode.

That Supreme Divine Personality, O Pritha's son, is the only ONE worthy of achieving by unswerving devotion; In whom all beings abide and who pervades in every being. The periods that signify whether a

Yogi will return or not return to this mortal realm after departing here, is as follows, O best of Bharats.

Sunlit moon's fortnight [Shukla paksh] & six months of sun's northward movement [Uttarayan]; departing during this period, the knowledgeable Yogis go to the Eternal. Foggy dark fortnight [Krishna Paksh] & six months of sun's southward movement [Dakshinayan]; departing during this period, moonlit Yogis return to this mortal realm.

These two paths, Shukla & Krishna [Lit & Dark], are the eternal exits of realms; one leads to liberation [Moksh], while the other leads to rebirth. Knowing these two paths, O Pritha's son, Yogis are never deluded; so at all times remain devoted to Yoga, O Arjun.

Only after surpassing Vedic recitations, Yajna, Austerities, Charities; appreciating all the benefits therein, a Yogi finally achieves the Supreme Primeval Abode.

9. Raj Vidhya Yog

Lord Shri Krishna:

Now I shall reveal, inarguably the most profound knowledge with explanation, knowing which will save you from inauspiciousness.

Noble knowledge that is royally profound & purest; practical, virtuous, easily adaptable and infallible. Non-Believers of [Sanatan] Dharma, O tormentor of foes; will not attain Me, and remain bound to this mortal realm by rebirth.

I pervade this entire creation in My unmanifested form; All manifestations depend on Me, but I do not depend on them. Remaining independent of all manifestations, through my Divine Yoga; creating & sustaining them, yet remaining unaffected by them.

Just as the mighty winds exist everywhere within the sky; similarly, understand that all manifestations exist in Me. All manifested, O Kunti's son, in this creation merges into Me at the end of every Kalp [dusk of Brahma's Night] & recreated at the beginning [dawn of Brahma's Day].

Creation's my dominion, which I recreate time and time again; the whole aggregate of manifestations, resigned to their own inherent nature. Those actions [of recreation], O victor of wealth, do not bind Me; I remain indifferent and unaffected by those actions. Under My supervision, Nature creates everything that is movable & immovable; owing to which, O Kunti's son, this universe functions.

To the deluded, I am unrecognizable in this human form; they are unable to see My Divinity and know that I am the Lord of all Beings. They are mindlessly involved in harmful expectations, harmful actions, & harmful knowledge and behave as if possessed by fiendish & demonic nature.

The great Souls possessing godly nature, O Pritha's Son, worship Me with complete devotion, knowing Me to be the Creator. The great

Souls always glorify Me with determination; bow with devotion, and constantly worship Me. Others meditate upon Me through knowledge & wisdom; As a whole Me or in separate forms as multifaceted as the universe.

I am Kritu [Vedic ritual], I am Yajna [Fire-Sacrifice], I am Swadha [Oblation], I am the Aushadam [Medicinal herbs], I am Mantra [Chants], I am Ajyam [Clarified Butter], I am Agni [Sacred Fire], I am Hutam [Offering]. I am the Universal Father, Mother, Sustainer & Grandsire; The sacred syllable Omkar [Om/Aum] worth learning and the Vedas [Rig, Sama, Yajur].

I am the Ultimate Path, Sustainer, Lord, Witness, Abode, Refuge, and Friend; the Origin, End, Stratum, Storage & Imperishable Seed. My warmth makes rain that I withhold as clouds before allowing it to fall; I am immortality as well as death, I am matter as well as anti-matter, O Arjun.

Knowers of [three] Vedas, soma drinkers, worship Me to cleanse their sins through Yajna & reach Heavens; As a result of their pious deeds, upon reaching the realm of Indra they relish divine luxuries enjoyed by Demi-gods.

They [knowers of 3 Vedas] enjoy the spacious heaven, but upon exhausting their pious deeds return to this mortal realm; such knowers of [three] Vedas, desirous of enjoyments, keep circling back & forth. But those who devoutly meditate upon Me, only worshiping Me; My such staunch devotees are blessed with My never ending bliss.

Even those devotees who faithfully worship other Demi-gods, indirectly worship Me, O Kunti's son, however their methods are incorrect. As I alone am the Lord & beneficiary of all Yajnas; Those who do not realize this truth, they fall back to this mortal realm. Those who worship Demigods reach Demigods, those who worship Ancestors reach Ancestors, those who worship Mortals reach Mortals; My worshippers reach Me.

Leaf [Betel leaf], flower, fruit [or Betel-nut], or water whosoever offers Me; such sincere offering by a devout I accept readily. Whatever you do, eat, sacrifice [as oblation], donate and endure as austerities, O Kunti's son, dedicate them to Me. Doing so will liberate you from all, auspicious or inauspicious, results arising from your actions and as a liberated renunciated Yogi, you shall reach Me.

To Me all beings are equal, I am neither inimical nor partial to anyone; but those who worship Me with devotion, they are in Me & I in them. Even if a vilest sinner worships Me with true devotion; he should be regarded as a rightly resolved pious person. For soon he becomes a virtuous Soul eligible for Divine Path; O Kunti's son, know this, My devotees never perish.

If I am, O Pritha's son, sought as a refuge by sinners, women, traders and menials, they attain the Divine Path. Needless to say that pious Brahmins, pious Kingly Sages, transiting through this joyless world, were all devoted to Me.

Thinking about Me, devoted to Me, worshiping Me, bowing to Me; being completely absorbed in Me, surely you will come to Me.

10. Vibhuti Yog

Lord Shri Krishna:

Listen closely, O mighty-armed, to my Divine teachings; Since you are delighted with it, so desiring your welfare I shall speak.

Neither the Demigods know my origin nor the Sages, I am the origin of Demigods, Sages & everything. Who knows Me to be unborn, beginningless and Supreme Lord of the Universe, He is un-deluded amongst mortals and will be freed from all sins.

Reason, knowledge, non-delusion, forgiveness, truthfulness, restraint, serenity, joy, sorrow, life, death, fear & courage, non-violence, equanimity, benevolence, fame and infamy - All these various qualities in humans arise from Me alone.

The seven Maharishis [Great Sages] and the four Manus [progenitors of mankind], they were all wished into being by Me and are the progenitors of the people of this world. He who comprehends the divinity & the prowess of My glorious Yoga; is undoubtedly, steadily united with Me.

I am the originator of all creation and all its functions; hence the wise worship Me with loving devotion. Remembering Me, dedicating their life to create awareness about Me; They derive satisfaction in spreading My teachings to others.

To them [preachers], constantly immersed in My devotion out of love; I give them the divine knowledge to attain Me. I benevolently destroy the darkness of ignorance dwelling in them [preachers] by lighting the lamp of knowledge [in their hearts].

Arjun:

You are the Supreme Brahman, Supreme Destination, Supremely Pure, Eternal Divine Being, Primal, Unborn, and all-pervading God.

The one mentioned by the great sages like Narad, Asit, Deval, Vyas and also by your own admission to me.

I believe everything you told me, O slayer of Keshi, neither the Demigods nor the Demons, know your Divine form. Only you yourself know about yourself, O Supreme Being; Creator & Lord of all beings, God of the Demigods, Ruler of the Universe.

You alone can describe Your Divine opulences with which You pervade and reside in this whole Universe. O Master of Yoga, how shall I forever visualize You? Which aspect of Your various facets should I meditate upon? As you describe the Glories of Your Yoga, O Janardan, I again remain unsatiated and want to hear more of this nectar.

Lord Shri Krishna:

Sure, now I shall describe My divine attributes; but only the most prominent ones, O best of Kurus, because they are unlimited. I am the life force with which the heart beats, O Gudakesh [Arjun], I am the beginning, the middle and also the end of all beings.

Amongst the Sons of Aditi I am Vishnu; Amongst the luminous I am the Sun, Amongst the wind I am Marichi, Amongst Constellations I am the Moon. Sama Veda amongst Vedas, Indra amongst Demigods; Amongst senses the Mind, Cognizance amongst living beings.

Amongst Rudras I am Shankar, amongst demons Kuber; Amongst Vasus I am Agni [Fire-god], amongst mountains I am Meru. I am the Brihaspati amongst priests & chiefs, O Pritha's Son, amongst Generals I am Skanda, amongst reservoirs the Ocean.

Amongst the great sages I am Rishi Bhrigu, amongst mono-syllables Aum [OM]; Jap [repetition of mantras] amongst rituals, amongst immovable Himalayas. Amongst the trees I am Ashvattha [pipal], amongst the Divine Sages I am Narada; Amongst Gandharvas I am Chitraratha and amongst Siddhas I am Sage Kapil.

Amongst horses know Me as Uchchaishrava born from ocean churning [Sagar Manthan]; Amongst lordly elephants know Me as

Airavat and amongst men I am the King. Amongst weapons know Me as Vajra [thunderbolt], Kamdhenu amongst cows; Kandarp [Kaamdev] amongst progenitors & Vasuki amongst serpents.

Amongst snakes know Me as Anant, Varuna amongst water beings; Aryama amongst Pritris [departed ancestors] & Yama amongst moral codes. Lord of Death amongst enforcers. Amongst Daityas know Me as Prahlad, Time amongst reckoners; Lion amongst animals, Vainateya [Garud or Eagle] amongst birds.

Amongst moving know Me as wind, Rama amongst warriors; Dolphin amongst fish & Ganges amongst springs. Of the Worlds I am the origin, middle and end; O Arjun, amongst sciences, the science of Spirituality and the logical conclusion amongst debaters.

Amongst letters I am A, and the grammatical link between compounds; I am the everlasting Time, the multifaceted Sustainer. I am Death of all existence & I am also the Seed of all future generations; amongst feminine qualities I am fame, prosperity, eloquence, memory, wisdom, constancy, and forbearance.

I am Brihat-Sama amongst hymns of Sama Veda, Gayatri [mantra] amongst poetic meters; Margashish amongst months, Spring amongst seasons. I am the trickster amongst gamblers, splendor of splendid; Success of strugglers, virtue of virtuous.

Amongst the clan of Vrishnis I am Vasudeva; Dhananjay [Arjun] amongst Pandavas; Vyas amongst silent sages, Shukracharya amongst poets. Amongst staves I am scepter; strategy amongst ambitious; Silence amongst secrets, knowledge amongst wise.

I am the seed of all living beings, O Arjun, none moving or unmoving being exists without Me. Unlimited are My Divine Attributes, O tormentor of foes; the ones I mentioned is just a minuscule account of My Divinity. Whichever being that is glorious, prosperous, and powerful; know it to spring from but a spark of my splendor.

Apart from these, what good would it be knowing about My other Divine Attributes, O Arjun? Suffice to know that I pervade & sustain this whole Universe with just a fraction of My being.

11. Vishwaroop darshan Yog

Lord Shri Krishna:

Listen closely, O mighty-armed, to my Divine teachings; Since you are delighted with it, so desiring your welfare I shall speak.

Neither the Demigods know my origin nor the Sages, I am the origin of Demigods, Sages & everything. Who knows Me to be unborn, beginningless and Supreme Lord of the Universe, He is un-deluded amongst mortals and will be freed from all sins.

Reason, knowledge, non-delusion, forgiveness, truthfulness, restraint, serenity, joy, sorrow, life, death, fear & courage, non-violence, equanimity, benevolence, fame and infamy - All these various qualities in humans arise from Me alone.

The seven Maharishis [Great Sages] and the four Manus [progenitors of mankind], they were all wished into being by Me and are the progenitors of the people of this world. He who comprehends the divinity & the prowess of My glorious Yoga; is undoubtedly, steadily united with Me.

I am the originator of all creation and all its functions; hence the wise worship Me with loving devotion. Remembering Me, dedicating their life to create awareness about Me; They derive satisfaction in spreading My teachings to others.

To them [preachers], constantly immersed in My devotion out of love; I give them the divine knowledge to attain Me. I benevolently destroy the darkness of ignorance dwelling in them [preachers] by lighting the lamp of knowledge [in their hearts].

Arjun:

You are the Supreme Brahman, Supreme Destination, Supremely Pure, Eternal Divine Being, Primal, Unborn, and all-pervading God.

The one mentioned by the great sages like Narad, Asit, Deval, Vyas and also by your own admission to me.

I believe everything you told me, O slayer of Keshi, neither the Demigods nor the Demons, know your Divine form. Only you yourself know about yourself, O Supreme Being; Creator & Lord of all beings, God of the Demigods, Ruler of the Universe.

You alone can describe Your Divine opulences with which You pervade and reside in this whole Universe. O Master of Yoga, how shall I forever visualize You? Which aspect of Your various facets should I meditate upon? As you describe the Glories of Your Yoga, O Janardan, I again remain unsatiated and want to hear more of this nectar.

Lord Shri Krishna:

Sure, now I shall describe My divine attributes; but only the most prominent ones, O best of Kurus, because they are unlimited. I am the life force with which the heart beats, O Gudakesh [Arjun], I am the beginning, the middle and also the end of all beings.

Amongst the Sons of Aditi I am Vishnu; Amongst the luminous I am the Sun, Amongst the wind I am Marichi, Amongst Constellations I am the Moon. Sama Veda amongst Vedas, Indra amongst Demigods; Amongst senses the Mind, Cognizance amongst living beings.

Amongst Rudras I am Shankar, amongst demons Kuber; Amongst Vasus I am Agni [Fire-god], amongst mountains I am Meru. I am the Brihaspati amongst priests & chiefs, O Pritha's Son, amongst Generals I am Skanda, amongst reservoirs the Ocean.

Amongst the great sages I am Rishi Bhrigu, amongst mono-syllables Aum [OM]; Jap [repetition of mantras] amongst rituals, amongst immovable Himalayas. Amongst the trees I am Ashvattha [pipal], amongst the Divine Sages I am Narada; Amongst Gandharvas I am Chitraratha and amongst Siddhas I am Sage Kapil.

Amongst horses know Me as Uchchaishrava born from ocean churning [Sagar Manthan]; Amongst lordly elephants know Me as

Airavat and amongst men I am the King. Amongst weapons know Me as Vajra [thunderbolt], Kamdhenu amongst cows; Kandarp [Kaamdev] amongst progenitors & Vasuki amongst serpents.

Amongst snakes know Me as Anant, Varuna amongst water beings; Aryama amongst Pritris [departed ancestors] & Yama amongst moral codes. Lord of Death amongst enforcers. Amongst Daityas know Me as Prahlad, Time amongst reckoners; Lion amongst animals, Vainateya [Garud or Eagle] amongst birds.

Amongst moving know Me as wind, Rama amongst warriors; Dolphin amongst fish & Ganges amongst springs. Of the Worlds I am the origin, middle and end; O Arjun, amongst sciences, the science of Spirituality and the logical conclusion amongst debaters.

Amongst letters I am A, and the grammatical link between compounds; I am the everlasting Time, the multifaceted Sustainer. I am Death of all existence & I am also the Seed of all future generations; amongst feminine qualities I am fame, prosperity, eloquence, memory, wisdom, constancy, and forbearance.

I am Brihat-Sama amongst hymns of Sama Veda, Gayatri [mantra] amongst poetic meters; Margashish amongst months, Spring amongst seasons. I am the trickster amongst gamblers, splendor of splendid; Success of strugglers, virtue of virtuous.

Amongst the clan of Vrishnis I am Vasudeva; Dhananjay [Arjun] amongst Pandavas; Vyas amongst silent sages, Shukracharya amongst poets. Amongst staves I am scepter; strategy amongst ambitious; Silence amongst secrets, knowledge amongst wise.

I am the seed of all living beings, O Arjun, none moving or unmoving being exists without Me. Unlimited are My Divine Attributes, O tormentor of foes; the ones I mentioned is just a minuscule account of My Divinity. Whichever being that is glorious, prosperous, and powerful; know it to spring from but a spark of my splendor.

Apart from these, what good would it be knowing about My other Divine Attributes, O Arjun? Suffice to know that I pervade & sustain this whole Universe with just a fraction of My being.

Lord Shri Krishna:

Listen closely, O mighty-armed, to my Divine teachings; Since you are delighted with it, so desiring your welfare I shall speak.

Neither the Demigods know my origin nor the Sages, I am the origin of Demigods, Sages & everything. Who knows Me to be unborn, beginningless and Supreme Lord of the Universe, He is un-deluded amongst mortals and will be freed from all sins.

Reason, knowledge, non-delusion, forgiveness, truthfulness, restraint, serenity, joy, sorrow, life, death, fear & courage, non-violence, equanimity, benevolence, fame and infamy - All these various qualities in humans arise from Me alone.

The seven Maharishis [Great Sages] and the four Manus [progenitors of mankind], they were all wished into being by Me and are the progenitors of the people of this world. He who comprehends the divinity & the prowess of My glorious Yoga; is undoubtedly, steadily united with Me.

I am the originator of all creation and all its functions; hence the wise worship Me with loving devotion. Remembering Me, dedicating their life to create awareness about Me; They derive satisfaction in spreading My teachings to others.

To them [preachers], constantly immersed in My devotion out of love; I give them the divine knowledge to attain Me. I benevolently destroy the darkness of ignorance dwelling in them [preachers] by lighting the lamp of knowledge [in their hearts].

Arjun:

You are the Supreme Brahman, Supreme Destination, Supremely Pure, Eternal Divine Being, Primal, Unborn, and all-pervading God. The one mentioned by the great sages like Narad, Asit, Deval, Vyas and also by your own admission to me.

I believe everything you told me, O slayer of Keshi, neither the Demigods nor the Demons, know your Divine form. Only you yourself know about yourself, O Supreme Being; Creator & Lord of all beings, God of the Demigods, Ruler of the Universe.

You alone can describe Your Divine opulences with which You pervade and reside in this whole Universe. O Master of Yoga, how shall I forever visualize You? Which aspect of Your various facets should I meditate upon? As you describe the Glories of Your Yoga, O Janardan, I again remain unsatiated and want to hear more of this nectar.

Lord Shri Krishna:

Sure, now I shall describe My divine attributes; but only the most prominent ones, O best of Kurus, because they are unlimited. I am the life force with which the heart beats, O Gudakesh [Arjun], I am the beginning, the middle and also the end of all beings.

Amongst the Sons of Aditi I am Vishnu; Amongst the luminous I am the Sun, Amongst the wind I am Marichi, Amongst Constellations I am the Moon. Sama Veda amongst Vedas, Indra amongst Demigods; Amongst senses the Mind, Cognizance amongst living beings.

Amongst Rudras I am Shankar, amongst demons Kuber; Amongst Vasus I am Agni [Fire-god], amongst mountains I am Meru. I am the Brihaspati amongst priests & chiefs, O Pritha's Son, amongst Generals I am Skanda, amongst reservoirs the Ocean.

Amongst the great sages I am Rishi Bhrigu, amongst mono-syllables Aum [OM]; Jap [repetition of mantras] amongst rituals, amongst immovable Himalayas. Amongst the trees I am Ashvattha [pipal], amongst the Divine Sages I am Narada; Amongst Gandharvas I am Chitraratha and amongst Siddhas I am Sage Kapil.

Amongst horses know Me as Uchchaishrava born from ocean churning [Sagar Manthan]; Amongst lordly elephants know Me as Airavat and amongst men I am the King. Amongst weapons know Me as Vajra [thunderbolt], Kamdhenu amongst cows; Kandarp [Kaamdev] amongst progenitors & Vasuki amongst serpents.

Amongst snakes know Me as Anant, Varuna amongst water beings; Aryama amongst Pritris [departed ancestors] & Yama amongst moral codes. Lord of Death amongst enforcers. Amongst Daityas know Me as Prahlad, Time amongst reckoners; Lion amongst animals, Vainateya [Garud or Eagle] amongst birds.

Amongst moving know Me as wind, Rama amongst warriors; Dolphin amongst fish & Ganges amongst springs. Of the Worlds I am the origin, middle and end; O Arjun, amongst sciences, the science of Spirituality and the logical conclusion amongst debaters.

Amongst letters I am 'A', and the grammatical link between compounds; I am the everlasting Time, the multifaceted Sustainer. I am Death of all existence & I am also the Seed of all future generations; amongst feminine qualities I am fame, prosperity, eloquence, memory, wisdom, constancy, and forbearance.

I am Brihat-Sama amongst hymns of Sama Veda, Gayatri [mantra] amongst poetic meters; Margashish amongst months, Spring amongst seasons. I am the trickster amongst gamblers, splendor of splendid; Success of strugglers, virtue of virtuous.

Amongst the clan of Vrishnis I am Vasudeva; Dhananjay [Arjun] amongst Pandavas; Vyas amongst silent sages, Shukracharya amongst poets. Amongst staves I am scepter; strategy amongst ambitious; Silence amongst secrets, knowledge amongst wise.

I am the seed of all living beings, O Arjun, none moving or unmoving being exists without Me. Unlimited are My Divine Attributes, O tormentor of foes; the ones I mentioned is just a minuscule account of My Divinity. Whichever being that is glorious, prosperous, and powerful; know it to spring from but a spark of my splendor.

Apart from these, what good would it be knowing about My other Divine Attributes, O Arjun? Suffice to know that I pervade & sustain this whole Universe with just a fraction of My being.

12. Bhakti Yog

Arjun:

Between Your ardent devotees, which are expert Yogis, those who worship You [as an idol] or those who worship Your Invincible Unmanifested form?

Lord Shri Krishna:

Those who can constantly meditate upon Me by visualizing Me [as an idol], those devotees I consider highly endowed Souls.

But those who worship the formless aspect of the Absolute Truth, the Invincible, the Indefinable, the Unmanifested, the All-pervading, the Unimaginable, the Immutable, the Eternal, & the immoveable by restraining their senses and being even-minded everywhere, such persons, engaged in the welfare of all beings, also attain Me.

It is tumultuous to bring the mind to adapt the Unmanifested, because Unmanifested is difficult to visualize by the [manifested] embodied [humans]. But those who dedicate all their activities as an act of worship to Me with undivided devotion. I deliver them from the ocean of this mortal realm without delay, O Pritha's son, those who idolize Me.

By visualizing Me the mind is fixated in Me, Once fixated in Me your mind thereafter would never doubt. If you are unable to visualize Me steadily; Then keep practicing Yoga and soon you will form the habit, O winner of wealth.

If you are unable to neither meditate nor practice [Yoga], then perform actions for My sake and you shall gain perfection. And if even that [acting for My sake] is not possible, seeking refuge in My Yoga, perform all your tasks selflessly.Knowledge is better than practice, meditation is better than knowledge, better than meditation is being selfless, as it speedily leads to peace.

[Those who are] hateless, friendly & kind towards all beings, without proprietorship, egoless, equipoised in happiness or sadness, forgiving, content, such determined Yogis, dedicated to Me in mind & reason, such devotees are dear to Me.

With whom the world is at ease and who is at ease with the world, free from pleasures, displeasures, jealousy, fear and worry, such a one is dear to Me. Un-expectant, un-cunningly clever, not indifferent to miseries of others; Selflessly motivated, such a devotee is dear to Me. Who is neither edgy, nor loathing, nor lamenting, nor craving; who is not a blindingly superstitious follower, he is dear to Me.

Impartial to friend or enemy, fame or infamy. Impartial to winter or summer, joy or sorrow, favorable or unfavorable associates; Patiently accept praise or insult while remaining reticent. Never hold grudges, such a devotee is dear to Me. Whosoever faithfully follows this immortal guiding principles of Dharma, as taught, are exceedingly dear to Me.

13. Kshetra Kshetragya Yog

Arjun:

O Keshava, I wish to understand what is Prakriti & Purusha, what is Kshetra, who is Kshetrajna? I also wish to know what true knowledge is and its goal?

Lord Shri Krishna:

This body, O Kunti's son, is the Kshetra [field of activities] and the one within [Soul] who knows it is called the Kshetrayajna [knower of the field]. I am the knower of all fields [of every being], O scion of Bharat, understanding the knower [Me] & the field [self] is true knowledge in My view. The field [this body], its nature, its transformations, and its causes; what is the role of field-knower and his powers, I will now describe them.

Great sages have sung the truth about the field and the knower of the field in many ways. It has been stated in various Vedic hymns, and especially revealed in the Brahma Sutra, with sound logic and conclusive evidence.

The great elements, reason, egoism, and the unmanifest, Senses ten plus one and five pastures of the senses. Affection, aversion, joy & sorrow, awareness & fortitude, this together has been briefly described as the field in its transformations.

Humility, simplicity, non-violence, forbearance, uprightness, devotion to teacher, purity, stability and self-control. Indifference to objects of senses, and absence of egoism, thinking about the demerits of birth, death, decay, sickness and sorrow.

Non-attachment and absence of [blind] affection for son, wife and home. Constant even-mindedness in occurrence of the desired or the undesired. Unerring devotion to Me by unswerving Yoga, living in a quiet quarter, and distaste in mixing with people. Constancy in learning the truth about self and reflecting on that truth; this is called knowledge, everything that is opposite to it is ignorance.

I shall now explain the knowable, knowing which you will enjoy immortality. The Beginningless is the Supreme Brahman, He is said to be neither being nor not-being. [The Supreme Brahman] has hands, feet, eyes, heads and mouths everywhere; listens to everything that is happening everywhere in this Universe.

Perceiving every sensory detail, even though being devoid of any senses; independent of any necessities or attributes, yet enjoys everything. Within and without all moving and also unmoving beings, subtlety incomprehensible. He is faraway, yet nearby. Indivisible yet present separately in all beings, He is also their Sustainer, Devourer and Creator.

He is the source of light in all luminaries, and is entirely beyond the darkness of ignorance. He is knowledge, the object of knowledge, and the goal of knowledge. He dwells within the hearts of all living beings.

I have thus revealed to you the nature of the field, the meaning of knowledge, and the object of knowledge. Only My devotees can understand this in reality, and by doing so, they attain My divine nature.

Know that prakṛiti [material nature] and puruṣh [the individual Souls] are both beginningless. Also know that all transformations of the body and the three traits of nature are produced by transacting with the material nature. Nature is responsible for the agency of cause & effect and the self is responsible for enjoying its pleasures & pains.

When the purush [individual Soul] seated in prakriti [the material nature] desires to enjoy the three gunas [traits], attachment to them becomes the cause of its birth in superior and inferior wombs.

Spectator, Permitter, Supporter, Enjoyer, and Lord residing within is the ultimate controller known as the Supreme Soul. Whosoever understands the Soul, the Nature and its three traits, regardless of their present state, they shall not be reborn.

Some are able to realize the Soul within through meditation, some through knowledge and others through Karmayoga [selfless deeds]. Those who are unaware of any spiritual paths, but still worship [Me] by hearing from others, also cross over death by developing devotion.

Every being, whether animate or inanimate, comes into existence as a result of the union of the "field" and "Knower of the field", O strongest amongst Bharat. Present equally in all living beings is that Supreme Lord, The Imperishable amidst the perishable [bodies], those who realize this, see the truth.

Knowing that the Supreme exists equally in all living beings, one does not hurt others, knowing that by hurting others, he is only hurting himself, only such Souls reach salvation. All actions are really performed by the body under the influence of three traits of nature, and who knows that the embodied Soul is just a non-actor, sees the truth.

When he sees diversity of beings rooted in unity and its evolution from the same, then he becomes Brahman-like. The Supreme Soul is imperishable, without beginning, and devoid of traits of nature, O Kunti's son. Although situated within the body, It neither acts, nor is It tainted by material nature.

Like the subtle space, which upholds everything yet remains untainted, similarly the all-pervading Soul in everybody remains untainted. Just as one sun illumines this whole world, so does the field-dweller [Soul] illumines the whole field [body], O Bharat.

Those who perceive the distinction between the 'Field' [Body] and the 'Knower of the body' [Soul] through the eyes of this knowledge and know how to liberate themselves from the three traits of nature, attain the Supreme.

14. Guna Traya Vibhag Yog

Lord Shri Krishna:

I shall once again explain to you the supreme wisdom, the best of all knowledge; by knowing which, all the great saints attained the highest perfection.

Those who have Surrendered & imbibed in this knowledge, are neither materialized nor tormented at the time of recreation or dissolution [pralay]. The nature [prakṛiti] is the womb.I impregnate it, wherefrom all living beings are born.

Every being, O Kunti's son, irrespective of their form is born from the womb of mother Nature and I am the seeding father. Born along are the three traits of Nature Satva, Rajas, & Tamas, O mighty armed, that envelop the unchangeable dweller [Soul] in a body.

Of the three traits of Nature, Satva due to its purity, is illumining and harmless; associating with Satva unites one with joy and knowledge, O Sinless. Associating with Rajas breeds temptations and desires, O Kunti's son, which binds the Soul, through attachment to fruitive actions. Association with Tamas breeds ignorance and mesmerizes everybody, and binds [the Soul] through listlessness, indolence and sleep, O Bharat.

Satva unites the Soul with joy, Rajas unites the Soul with fruitive actions, O Bharat, Tamas first blurs knowledge and then unites the Soul with lethargy. When Rajas and Tamas are overpowered, Satva prevails, O Bharat, when Satva and Tamas are overpowered, Rajas prevails and when Satva and Rajas are overpowered, Tamas prevails.

When all sense organs emanate radiance through knowledge and wisdom, know that Satva is predominant; greed, activity, initiation of action, anxiety, and craving appear when Rajas is predominant, O Arjun, darkness, inactivity, heedlessness and delusion arises when Tamas predominates, O scion of Kuru.

If the Soul that departs from the body when Satva is predominant, it achieves the highest realms of scholars. If the Soul departs when Rajas , it is reborn among other actionists, if the Soul departs when Tamas is predominant, then it is reborn through wombs of the less intelligent.

Outcome of action performed, when Satva is predominant is pure and stainless, when Rajas is predominant is grief, when Tamas is predominant leads to unintelligence. Satva raises knowledge, Rajas raises greed, and Tamas raises unintelligence, delusion and mindlessness.

Satvic Souls rise to higher realms, Rajasic Souls remain in the middle [mortal realm of earth], and those Souls with lower qualities of Tamas fall low into unintelligent species. Only upon realizing that it is none other but these traits of Nature that compels one to act as per their predominance, does one merges with me.

Only after rising above the three traits of Nature, the Soul is freed from birth, death, decay, and sorrow to attain immortality.

Arjun:

O Lord, what are the features of those who have surpassed the three traits of Nature? How do they conduct themselves? How does one rise above these three traits of Nature?

Lord Shri Krishna:

Neither illumination [Satva], nor activity [Rajas] or delusion [Tamas] , O Pandava, affects such a person, he neither abhors it when any of these traits are present, nor craves for it when they are absent.

Indifferent and uninfluenced he remains unmoved and fully aware that it is the three traits of Nature that are causing all the commotion. Equipoised in joy or sorrow, self-aware, valuing equally a lump of clay, stone or gold, pleasure or displeasure, enduring equally fame or infamy

Enduring equally, praise or insult, treating equally a friend or a foe, renouncing all enterprise, he is called a 'Gunateet', the one who has risen above the three traits of Nature. Whosoever serves Me with sincere devotion rises above the three traits of Nature and is fit to attain Brahma [immortality]. 54

Because for the Brahman [the immortal], Eternal and Infinite, I am the abode, as I am the abode for the Eternal Dharma and of the Absolute Bliss.

15. Purushottam Yog

Lord Shri Krishna:

Life is like a fig tree, whose roots originate at the top and branch downwards, as recited by the knowers from leaves of the Vedas.

This fig tree's branches spread upwards as well as downwards and are nourished by the traits of Nature; sensual organs are its buds, the Karmas [actions of the sensual organs] form the network of rootlets that binds [the Soul] to this human world.

This fig tree's real form, origin, end or existence is imperceptible, but this deep rooted Ashvattha [fig tree] must be cut down with the strong weapon of detachment and then that ultimate destination can be sought, reaching which there is no returning to this cycle of birth & death; even I seek refuge in that same Primeval Being, out of whom this life originated long ago.

Without pride or delusion, having won over the ills of attachments; enlightened and free from desires and contradictions of joy & sorrow, the wise [Soul] reaches that Eternal Goal [Moksha]. Neither by sun, nor by moon, nor fire is My Supreme Abode illuminated. Having gone There, no one returns to this material world again.

Every eternal embodied Souls in this mortal world are My fragments, which are bound here due to their attraction toward the traits of Nature through their senses. When an embodied Soul assumes or relinquishes a body, it brings along the residue sensual attractions with it from its old shell, like the wind carries the scent faraway from its origin.

[The embodied Soul] Through ears, eyes, skin, tongue, nose and mind enjoys the objects. It [the embodied Soul] migrates, resides, or gets entangled under the influence of three traits of Nature; the wise see this through the lens of knowledge, but the ignorant cannot. Striving Yogis too are able to realize that it [the Soul] is enshrined within their bodies. But, those who are confused by ego are unable to realize it, even after striving.

Understand that the light in the sun which illuminates the whole world, the light in the moon and in the fire is My radiance. Enclosing the earth I support every being with My energy, I nourish and rejuvenate all with the nectar of life at night.

Becoming digestive fire in the stomach of all living beings and with the aid of inhaling and exhaling breath, I digest the food in four steps. I am enshrined in everybody's heart, from Me comes knowledge, memory, forgetfulness. It is I, that is to be learnt through Vedas, as well as its creator and its scholar.

Duality exists in every being of this realm, there is a part of this duality which lasts and another which does not; all that is born is mortal and one that is imperishable is immortal. But besides these dualities, there is the imperishable Divine Supreme Personality, who pervades all three realms and sustains them.

Because I am transcendental, beyond both the perishable and imperishable and the greatest; I am celebrated both in the world and in the Vedas as that Supreme Person. The wise who know Me as the Supreme Divine Personality, knows that I am all there is to know and hence worships Me whole-heartedly, O scion of Bharat.

This is the most profound knowledge of the Vedic scriptures, O sinless one, and it is disclosed to you by Me. Whosoever understands this will become wise, and his endeavors will know perfection, O scion of Bharat.

16. Daivasura Sampad Vibhag Yog

Lord Shri Krishna:

Fearlessness, self-purification through Satva lifestyle, gaining knowledge, charity, continence, Yajna [fire sacrifice], studying scriptures, austerity, and moral righteousness, non-violence, truth, non-anger, renunciation, serenity, non-pettiness, compassion towards all beings, non-covetousness, gentleness, modesty, determined, lustrous, forgiving, courageous, cleanliness, loyalty, non-hubristic are the virtues of those born with divine qualities, O scion of Bharat.

Hypocrisy, ostentatious, vain, short-tempered, insolent, unintelligent, O son of Pritha, are found in those born with demonic qualities.

The divine qualities lead to liberation [Moksha], while the demonic qualities lead to bondage [of birth & death], worry not O Pandava, you are born with divine qualities. Two types of people exist in this world, the divine and the demonic; I have already described the divine, now I shall describe the demonic type, O Pritha's son, so listen.

The demonic cannot differentiate between proper or improper, they lack cleanliness, good conduct, and honesty. They believe that this world is unreal, without a purpose, without a God, everybody's born from and for lust and nothing else. With that belief they not only destroy themselves, but their narrow mindedness results in cruel deeds that threaten the well-being of the entire world.

Resigned to insatiable lust, full of hypocrisy, ostentatiousness, and hubris, the demoniac cling to their false tenets. Thus deluded, they are attracted to the impermanence and work with impure resolve. They are obsessed with ceaseless anxieties that ends only with their death.

Completely convinced that lust and accumulation of wealth for lust is the highest purpose of life. Bound by hundreds of desires driven by lust and anger, they seek to hoard riches for sensual enjoyment by unlawful means.

Demonic people believe that now they have accumulated some wealth which will fulfill their particular desire, tomorrow they shall beget more wealth and fulfill other desires; after they have killed an enemy, they think they can kill any adversary, they feel like they are Gods, all powerful, the perfect enjoyer and happy.

Demonic people believe that just because they are wealthy they are entitled, because they have connections with the affluent, there is none other like them, they perform sacrifices, give charity and make merry. They are confounded by manifold desires, caught in the net of delusion, entangled in sensual-enjoyments, they fall into foul hell.

Such self-conceited and self-righteous demonic people, full of pride and arrogance, perform ostentatious sacrifices for showing off, disregarding the rules of the scriptures. Blinded by ego, power, haughtiness, lust, and anger, the demonic hurt Me, who is present within their own body and in the bodies of other beings they kill.

These cruel, hateful, vilest and vicious of human beings, I hurl them back into demonic wombs in this mortal world, time and again. Such unintelligent demonic people, birth after birth, are born through the demonic wombs and remain oblivious about Me, O Kunti's son, reaching the most abominable states of existence.

Three gates lead to this hell of self-destruction of the Soul - Lust, anger, and greed. Therefore, one should abandon all three. The man who has escaped these three gates of hell, O Kunti's son, performs acts conducive to self-realization and thus gradually attains the supreme destination. He who disregards scriptural injunctions and acts according to his own whims attains neither perfection, nor happiness, nor the supreme destination.

Therefore, let the scriptures be your guiding principle in determining what should be done and what should not be done.

Knowing what has been prescribed in the scriptures you have to act accordingly.

59

17 Shraddha Traya Vibhag Yog

Arjun:

Those who unknowingly do not follow scriptures, yet worship with great reverence, O Krishna, is their intention Satvic, Rajasic or Tamasic?

Lord Shri Krishna:

Every human being is born with an inherent faith, it could be any one of these three - Satvic, Rajasic, or Tamasic. Let Me explain. Each individual's faith is according to his inherent essence from his previous life, O scion of Bharat, his faith shapes him and he shapes his faith.

Those born with Satvic traits worship Divine Gods, Rajasic worship Yakshas & Rakshasas, Tamasic worship the Ghosts & Spirits. Those who undergo severe austerities and penances contradicting the scriptures, performing them out of pride and egoism, they are impelled by lust and attachment. These senseless men torture the aggregate of the Elements in their body as well as Me dwelling within, are of demonic trait.

Even the love for food in everybody is of three types, as is the inclination for Yajna, austerity, and charity. Let Me explain their differences.

Food which grants longevity, mental peace, strength, immunity, cheerfulness, and satisfaction that is juicy, greasy, filling, and tasty is dear to the Satvic. Food which is bitter, sour, salty, spicy, pungent, dry or charred causes unhappiness, grief, and disease is dear to Rajasic. Food which is cold, overcooked, foul-smelling, stale and leftover is dear to Tamasic.

Yajna performed without wishing for a boon, as prescribed and as one's duty is Satvic. But when a Yajna is performed for a benefit or for ostentation, O scion of Bharat, it becomes Rajasic. Yajna performed unconventionally, without distributing food, or without chanting mantras, without donation or devotion is considered Tamasic.

When worship of the Supreme Lord, the Brahmins, the spiritual master, and the learned is done with the observance of cleanliness, modesty, continence, and harmlessness then that is the austerity of the body. Words that are unoffending, true, pleasing and positive along with regular study of Scriptures is austerity of speech. Mental serenity, benevolence, silence, self-control and purity in thought is the austerity of the mind.

This trio of austerities practiced with ardent faith without desiring a reward by the devout is Satvic. Austerity that is performed ostentatiously for gaining respect and recognition is Rajasic. Its benefits are unsteady and transitory. Austerity that is performed by those with foolish notions, and which involves torturing the self or harming others, is Tamasic.

Charity given out of duty, without expecting anything in return, at a proper time and place, and to a worthy person is Satvic. Charity given expecting something in return or with an intention of some kind of reward, or reluctantly is called Rajasic. Charity given at the wrong place and at the wrong time for an unworthy cause, with a grudge is Tamasic.

"Om Tat Sat" is the symbolic representation of the Supreme Absolute Truth. From which the priests, the scriptures, and the sacrifices came into being at creation. Therefore, the chanters of the Vedas who while performing Yajna, charity and penance in accordance with scriptural regulations always begin by uttering Om.

Who do not expect any rewards, but seek to be free from material entanglements, utter the word "Tat" along with acts of austerity, Yajna, and charity. The Absolute Truth is the objective of devotional sacrifice, and it is indicated by the word 'Sat', O Pritha's son. When 'Sat' is uttered for Yajna, austerity, or charity it denotes eternal truth and a complete devotion towards Me and that action is performed for My sake.

Any Yajna, charity, austerity, or penance performed without faith in the Supreme, O Pritha's son, is impermanent. It is asat [untrue] and is worthless both in this life and the next.

18. Moksha Sanyaas Yog

Arjun:

O mighty-armed, I wish to understand the essence and distinction between 'Sannyas' and 'Tyaga', O killer of the Kesi demon, master of the senses.

Lord Shri Krishna:

Renunciation of actions done for rewards is called 'Sannyas' by the knowledgeable, and abandoning the ownership of the results of all actions is called 'Tyag' by the wise. Some scholars believe that all actions are impure and should be renounced. However, some believe that Yajna, charity and austerity should not be renounced.

My conclusion about 'Tyag', O scion of Bharat, O tiger amongst men, is that there are three types 'Tyag'. Yajna, charity and austerity should not be renounced, but performed, because these have a purifying effect on the intellect.

All these Yajna, charities & austerities should be performed without attachment or any expectation of a reward or ownership. They should be performed as a matter of duty, O Pritha's son, That is My supreme verdict.

Prescribed duties should never be renounced. If one gives up his prescribed duties because of delusion, then such renunciation is said to be Tamasic.

Giving up prescribed duties of Yajna, charity, and austerity deeming that they are too cumbersome or physically strenuous is 'Tyag' [renunciation] that is Rajasic. Never benefit from such 'Tyag'. When one performs his prescribed duties of Yajna, charity, and austerity as one's responsibility and renounces the desire of a reward or ownership, O Arjun, then that 'Tyag' [renunciation] is said to be Satvic.

Who has neither aversion to discomforting nor a preference to a comforting duty, is without doubt an established Satvic 'Tyagi'. It is indeed impossible for an embodied being to give up all activities. But he who renounces the desire for a reward and the ownership of his actions is a true 'Tyagi'.

Desirable, undesirable, or mixed are the three types of rewards & results that await the non-'Tyagis' [non-renouncers] after their death, but none for the 'Tyagis'.

Now learn from Me the five factors, O mighty-armed, that have been mentioned for the accomplishment of all actions in the doctrine of Sankhya. The [physical] body, the doer [intellect], sense organs, particular [sense organ's] function and fate being the fifth. Whatever action a body performs, whether just or unjust, either physically, through speech or by thought, these five [body, intellect, sense organs and their individual functions and fate] causes it.

Therefore one who thinks himself the only doer, not considering the five factors, is certainly not very intelligent and cannot see things as they are. Whoever is free from ownership and motive for his actions, even though he may slay living beings, he neither kills nor is he bound by his actions.

Perception, perceived, and perceiver are the three motivators; The senses, the act and the doer are the three constituents of action. Knowledge, action, and doer, differ according to their inherent Guna [Traits: Satva, Rajas, & Tamas] as described in Sankhya, learn their true nature also.

That knowledge by which the indivisible indestructible Supreme One is seen in all living entities, even though they are divided into innumerable forms, that knowledge is Satvic. That knowledge by which one sees that in every different body there is a different type of living entity is Rajasic. That knowledge which is fixated that there is nothing beyond this physical body, lacking in true insight and petty is Tamasic.

The action which is performed as a duty, without ownership, free from affection or aversion, and without a desire for a reward is Satvic. The action which is performed with great effort by one seeking to gratify his desires, and enacted from a sense of false ego, is Rajasic. The action which is performed in delusion, disregarding scriptural injunctions, heedless of its consequences, violent and harmful to others is Tamasic.

The doer who is free from ownership and ego, filled with courage and enthusiasm, unaffected by success or failure is Satvic. The doer who is ambitious, seeks rewards for his actions, greedy, heartless, impure, subject to joy and sorrow, is Rajasic. The doer who is fickle, vulgar, obstinate, deceptive, destructive, insolent, despondent and procrastinating is Tamasic.

Now I will tell you in detail about the different kinds of understanding and reasoning, according to the three traits of nature, O victor of wealth.

That understanding by which one knows what ought to be done and what ought not to be done, what is to be feared and what is not to be feared, what is binding and what is liberating is Satvic, O Pritha's son. That understanding which cannot distinguish between dharma and adharma, between action and inaction, O Pritha's son, is Rajasic. That understanding which considers adharma to be dharma and vice-versa under the spell of illusion and darkness, and perverts everything, O Pritha's son, is Tamasic.

That reasoning which is unshakable, which is sustained with steadfastness towards yoga, and which thus controls the activities of the mind, life and senses is Satvic determination, O Pritha's son. That reasoning which is held fast by religious activities for a reward, pleasures and wealth, O Arjun, is Rajasic. That reasoning which does not go beyond dreaming, fearfulness, lamentation, vanity and delusion – such unintelligent reasoning, O Pritha's son, is Tamasic.

Now I will describe the three kinds of happiness, O best of Bharats, conditioned by which the Soul revels, ending all sorrows.

That happiness which in the beginning seems like poison but turns out to be like nectar in the end, which awakens self-realization by the mind is Satvic. That happiness which is derived by the pleasures of senses from the union with their objects and which appears like nectar at first but turns out to be poison at the end is Rajasic. That happiness which is blind to self-realization, which is delusion from beginning to end and which arises from sleep, laziness and illusion is Tamasic.

Neither on earth nor in the higher realms amongst the demigods or others, is there an entity free from the effect of the three traits of Nature. Brahmins, Kshatriyas, Vaishyas, and Shudras, O tormentor of foes, are born as per their [previous life's] karmas, as well as separated by the influence of their inherent Guna [traits].

Peacefulness, self-control, austerity, purity, tolerance, honesty, knowledge, wisdom and piety – these are the indicative attributes of a Brahmin. Valor, strength, fortitude, strategic aptitude, courage in battle, philanthropy and leadership are the indicative attributes of a Kshatriya. Those who are naturally adept at farming, animal husbandry, trading, and commerce are Vaishyas. And those that serve society through their vocational talents are Shudras.

Only through dutiful and diligent execution of their respective duties does a being fulfill their destiny and achieve perfection, listen to how it's done. Who is the source of all beings and who is all-pervading, a man can attain perfection by performing one's role as His worship.

Better to perform one's own role, even if devoid of merit, than well-performing another's role, performing action consonant with one's aptitude man does not incur sin. An individual might view their duties as vain, O Kunti's son, however, they must not abandon them - for like smoke covers a fire, the true purpose fulfilled by their duties is oft-times hidden from their intellect. With mind detached from all yearning through self-realization, a man attains the highest perfection of acting without incurring karmas, by renunciation.

Having achieved that perfection, listen to how one attains Brahman, I will briefly explain to you, O Kunti's son, that which is the final stage of knowledge.

One becomes fit to attain Brahman when he or she possesses a purified intellect and firmly restrains the senses, abandoning sound and other objects of the senses, casting aside attraction and aversion. Such a person relishes solitude, eats lightly, controls body, mind, and speech, is ever engaged in meditation, and practices dispassion.

Free from egotism, violence, arrogance, desire, possessiveness of property, and selfishness, such a person, situated in tranquility, is fit for union with Brahman [Moksha]. One who is thus transcendentally situated at once realizes the Supreme Brahman and becomes fully joyful. He never laments or desires to have anything. He is equally disposed toward every living entity. In that state he attains pure devotion for Me.

By devotion one comes to know who & what I am in Truth. Then, by knowing My essence, My devotee merges with Me. Thus My devotees perform all their actions depending on Me, by My grace they attain everlasting and eternal state [Moksha].

Surrender all actions unto Me mentally, refuged in Yog of the intellect, keep your consciousness immersed in My devotion. By dedicating your devotion to Me, by My grace you shall overcome all obstacles and difficulties. But if, due to pride, you do not listen to My advice, you will perish.

If, motivated by pride, you say, 'You will not fight," your resolve will be futile, because your nature will compel you to fight. You may refuse to fight due to delusion, O Kunti's son, but bound by your inherent Karma & qualities of your nature's traits, you will choose fighting.

The Supreme Lord is situated in everyone's heart, O Arjun, but Maya [illusion formed by them due to their traits of Nature] drives them, like a driver driving a vehicle. O scion of Bharat, surrender unto Him completely. By His grace you will attain transcendental peace and the supreme and eternal abode.

Thus I have explained to you the profoundest of confidential knowledge. Deliberate over it deeply, and then do as you wish.

Listen to My most confidential supreme words, because you are My dear friend and they are for your benefit. Always think of Me, be devoted to Me, worship Me, and offer obeisance to Me. Doing so, you will certainly come to Me. This is My pledge to you, for you are very dear to Me.Give up every other activity and simply surrender unto Me alone. I shall liberate you from all sins; do not worry.

This confidential knowledge may never be explained to those who are not austere, or devoted, or engaged in devotional service, nor to one who is envious of Me.

Whosoever interprets and teaches this most profound doctrine to My devotees with supreme devotion in Me, will come to Me. There none is more dearer to Me than him [the interpreter & teacher] amongst men, neither will there ever be anyone else more dearer than him on earth.

And whosoever studies this sacred dialogue of ours, will be worshiping Me through Yajna of knowledge, this is My opinion. Whosoever listens to this profound knowledge whole heartedly and without ill feelings, after death will attain the blessed pious realms of the righteous.

Did you listen, O Pritha's son, with an attentive mind, is your delusion of ignorance been destroyed, O victor of wealth?

Arjun:

My delusion is destroyed and I have regained my senses by Thy grace, O Unwavering. There are no doubts left and I shall do Thy bidding.

Sanjay:

Thus have I heard the conversation of two great Souls, Krishna and Arjun. And so wonderful is that message that my hair is standing on end. By the mercy of Vyasa, I have heard this most confidential dialogue between the master of all mysticism, Krishna, who was speaking personally to Arjun. O King, as I repeatedly recall this wondrous and holy dialogue between Krishna and Arjun, I take pleasure, being thrilled at every moment. As I remember the wonderful form of Lord Krishna, I am struck with wonder more and more, and I rejoice again and again.

Wherever there is Krishna, the master of all mystics, and wherever there is Arjun, the supreme archer, there will also certainly be opulence, victory, extraordinary power, and morality. That is my opinion.

All Shlokas

Chapter 01

dhritarashtra uvacha dharma-kshetre kuru-kshetre samaveta yuyutsavah mamakah pandavashchaiva kimakurvata sanjaya

Dhritarashtra says: O Sanjay, after gathering on the holy field of Kurukshetra with the desire to fight, what did my sons and the sons of Pandu do ?

sanjaya uvacha drishtva tu pandavanikam vyudham duryodhanastada acharyamupasangamya raja vachanamabravit

Sanjay replies: On observing the Pandava army standing in military formation, King Duryodhan approached his teacher Dronacharya, and spoke the following words.

pashyaitam pandu-putranam acharya mahatim chamum vyudham drupada-putrena tava shishyena dhimata

Duryodhan says: Respected teacher! Behold the mighty army of Pandu's sons, so expertly arrayed for battle by your own gifted disciple, the son of Drupad.

atra shura maheshvasa bhimarjuna-sama yudhi yuyudhano viratashcha drupadashcha maha-rathah

Behold in their ranks are many powerful archers, like Bheem, Arjuna, Yuyudhan, Virat, and Drupad who are all Maharathi.

dhrishtaketushchekitanah kashirajashcha viryavan purujit kuntibhojashcha shaibyashcha nara-pungavah

There are also accomplished heroes like Dhrishtaketu, Chekitan, the gallant King of Kashi, Purujit, Kuntibhoj, and Shaibya bull amongst men.

yudhamanyushcha vikranta uttamaujashcha viryavan saubhadro draupadeyashcha sarva eva maha-rathah

In their ranks, they also have the courageous Yudhamanyu, the gallant Uttamauja, the son of Subhadra, and the sons of Draupadi, who are all great warriors.

asmakam tu vishishta ye tannibodha dwijottama nayaka mama sainyasya sanjnartham tanbravimi te

O the best of Reincarnates, hear too about the principal generals on our side, who are especially qualified to lead. These I now recount unto you.

bhavanbhishmashcha karnashcha kripashcha samitinjayah ashvatthama vikarnashcha saumadattis tathaiva cha

There are personalities like yourself, Bheeshma, Karna, Kripa, Ashwatthama, Vikarn, and Saumdatta's son [Bhurishrava], who are ever victorious in battle.

anye cha bahavah shura madarthe tyaktajivitah nana-shastra-praharanah sarve yuddha-visharadah

Also, there are many other heroic warriors, who are prepared to lay down their lives for my sake. They are all skilled in the art of warfare, and equipped with various kinds of weapons.

aparyaptam tadasmakam balam bhishmabhirakshitam paryaptam tvidametesham balam bhimabhirakshitam

The strength of our army is unlimited and we are safely marshalled by Grandsire Bheeshma, while the strength of the Pandava army, carefully marshalled by Bheem is limited.

ayaneshu cha sarveshu yatha-bhagamavasthitah bhishmamevabhirakshantu bhavantah sarva eva hi

Therefore, I call upon all the generals of the Kaurava army now to give full support to Grandsire Bheeshma, even as you defend your respective strategic points.

tasya sanjanayan harsham kuru-vriddhah pitamahah simha-nadam vinadyochchaih shankham dadhmau pratapavan

Then, the grand old man of the Kuru dynasty, the glorious patriarch Bheeshma, blew his conch shell like a lion's roar, bringing joy to Duryodhan.

tatah shankhashcha bheryashcha panavanaka-gomukhah sahasaivabhyahanyanta sa shabdastumulo 'bhavat

Thereafter, conches, kettledrums, bugles, trumpets, and horns suddenly blared forth, and their combined sound was overwhelming.

tatah shvetairhayairyukte mahati syandane sthitau madhavah pandavashchaiva divyau shankhau pradadhmatuh

Then, from amidst the Pandava army, seated in a glorious chariot drawn by white horses, Madhav and Arjun blew their Divine conch shells.

panchajanyam hrishikesho devadattam dhananjayah paundram dadhmau maha-shankham bhima-karma vrikodarah

Hrishikesh blew his conch shell, called Panchajanya, and Arjun blew the Devadutta. Bheem, the voracious eater and performer of herculean tasks, blew his mighty conch, called Paundra.

anantavijayam raja kunti-putro yudhishthirah nakulah sahadevashcha sughosha-manipushpakau

King Yudhishthir blew the Anantavijay, while Nakul and Sahadev blew the Sughosh and Manipushpak respectively

kashyashcha parameshvasah shikhandi cha maha-rathah dhrishtadyumno viratashcha satyakish chaparajitah drupado draupadeyashcha sarvashah prithivi-pate

The excellent archer and king of Kashi, the great warrior Shikhandi, Dhrishtadyumna, Virat, and the invincible Satyaki

saubhadrashcha maha-bahuh shankhandadhmuh prithak prithak

Drupad, the five sons of Draupadi, and the mighty-armed Abhimanyu, son of Subhadra, all blew their respective conch shells, O Ruler of the earth.

sa ghosho dhartarashtranam hridayani vyadarayat nabhashcha prithivim chaiva tumulo abhyanunadayan

The terrific sound thundered across the sky and the earth, and shattered the hearts of your sons, O Dhritarasthra.

atha vyavasthitan drishtva dhartarashtran kapi-dhwajah pravritte shastra-sampate dhanurudyamya pandavah hrishikesham tada vakyam idam aha mahi-pate

At that time, the son of Pandu, Arjun, who had the insignia of Hanuman on the flag of his chariot, took up his bow. Seeing your sons arrayed against him, O King, Arjun says to Shri Krishna, O Infallible One, please take the chariot inbetween both armies.

yavadetan nirikshe 'ham yoddhu-kaman avasthitan kairmaya saha yoddhavyam asmin rana-samudyame

so that I may look at the warriors arrayed for battle, whom I must fight in this great combat.

yotsyamanan avekshe 'ham ya ete 'tra samagatah dhartarashtrasya durbuddher yuddhe priya-chikirshavah

I desire to see those who have come here to fight on the side of the evil-minded son of Dhritarasthra, wishing to please him.

sanjaya uvacha evam ukto hrishikesho gudakeshena bharata senayor ubhayor madhye sthapayitva rathottamam bhishma-drona-pramukhatah sarvesham cha mahi-kshitam uvacha partha pashyaitan samavetan kurun iti

Sanjay says: O Dhritarasthra, having thus been addressed by Arjun, the conqueror of sleep, Shri Krishna then drew the magnificent chariot between the two armies. In the presence of Bheeshma, Dronacharya, and all the other kings, Shri Krishna says: O Pritha's son, behold these Kurus gathered here.

tatrapashyat sthitan parthah pitrin atha pitamahan acharyan matulan bhratrin putran pautran sakhims tatha shvashuran suhridash chaiva senayor ubhayor api

There, Arjun could see stationed in both armies, his fathers, grandfathers, teachers, maternal uncles, brothers, cousins, sons, nephews, grand-nephews, friends, fathers-in-law, and well-wishers.

tan samikshya sa kaunteyah sarvan bandhun avasthitan kripaya
parayavishto vishidann idam abravit

Seeing all his relatives present there, Arjun, the son of Kunti, was
overwhelmed with compassion, and with deep sorrow, spoke the
following words.

arjuna uvacha drishtvemam sva-janam krishna yuyutsum
samupasthitam sidanti mama gatrani mukham cha parishushyati
vepathush cha sharire me roma-harshash cha jayate

Arjun says: O Krishna, seeing my own kinsmen arrayed for battle
here and intent on killing each other, my limbs are giving way and my
mouth is drying up. My whole body shudders and my hair are standing
on ends.

gandivam sramsate hastat tvak chaiva paridahyate na cha
shaknomy avasthatum bhramativa cha me manah

My bow Gandeev is slipping from my hand, and my skin is burning
all over. My mind is in a quandary and whirling in confusion.

nimittani cha pashyami viparitani keshava na cha shreyo
'nupashyami hatva sva-janam ahave

I am unable to hold myself steady any longer. O Krishna, killer of
the Keshi demon, I only see omens of misfortune. I do not foresee how
any good can come from killing my own kinsmen in this battle.

na kankshe vijayam krishna na cha rajyam sukhani cha kim no
rajyena govinda kim bhogair jivitena va

O Krishna, I do not desire the victory, kingdom, or the happiness
accruing it

yesham arthe kankshitam no rajyam bhogah sukhani cha ta ime
'vasthita yuddhe pranams tyaktva dhanani cha

Of what avail will be a kingdom, pleasures, or even life itself, when
the very persons for whom we covet them, are standing before us for
battle?

acharyah pitarah putras tathaiva cha pitamahah matulah
shvashurah pautrah shyalah sambandhinas tatha

Teachers, fathers, sons, grandfathers, maternal uncles, grandsons, fathers-in-law, grand-nephews, brothers-in-law, and other kinsmen are present here.

etan na hantum ichchhami ghnato 'pi madhusudana api trailokya-rajyasya hetoh kim nu mahi-krite

O Madhusudan, Even if I get the dominion over the three worlds, let alone this Earth - I won't kill them.

nihatya dhartarashtran nah ka pritih syaj janardana papam evashrayed asman hatvaitan atatayinah

O Janardan, what pleasure will we derive from the sin of killing these desperado sons of Dhritarasthra?

tasman narha vayam hantum dhartarashtran sa-bandhavan sva-janam hi katham hatva sukhinah syama madhava

O Madhav, how can we hope to be happy by killing Dhritarashtra's sons and our own kinsmen?

yady apy ete na pashyanti lobhopahata-chetasah kula-kshaya-kritam dosham mitra-drohe cha patakam

They are overtaken by greed and see no wrong in annihilating their relatives or betraying their friends.

katham na jneyam asmabhih papad asman nivartitum kula-kshaya-kritam dosham prapashyadbhir janardana

Yet O Janardan, why should we, who can clearly see the crime in killing our kindred, not turn away from this sin?

kula-kshaye pranashyanti kula-dharmah sanatanah dharme nashte kulam kritsnam adharmo 'bhibhavaty uta

When a dynasty is destroyed, its traditions get vanquished, and the family strays from the path of religion.

adharmabhibhavat krishna pradushyanti kula-striyah strishu dushtasu varshneya jayate varna-sankarah

As a result, the family and its women are corrupted and distanced from their lineage, spawning tainted offspring.

sankaro narakayaiva kula-ghnanam kulasya cha patanti pitaro hy esham lupta-pindodaka-kriyah

The future generations born in such a family are from corrupted wombs and know not to respect their ancestors and to whom they will offer no obeisance.

doshair etaih kula-ghnanam varna-sankara-karakaih utsadyante jati-dharmah kula-dharmash cha shashvatah

And thus the future generations of a once great dynasty will bring about their own downfall by destroying the great values which they were themselves responsible for carrying forward.

utsanna-kula-dharmanam manushyanam janardana narake 'niyatam vaso bhavatityanushushruma

O Janardan [Krishna], I have heard from the learned that those who destroy family traditions dwell in hell for eternity.

aho bata mahat papam kartum vyavasita vayam yad rajya-sukha-lobhena hantum sva-janam udyatah

Alas! In our wisdom we see ourselves about to commit such a great sin of killing our kinsmen for a throne and luxuries it entails.

yadi mam apratikaram ashastram shastra-panayah dhartarashtra rane hanyus tan me kshemataram bhavet

I would rather have Dhritrashtra's sons find me unarmed on the battlefield that they may slay me

sanjaya uvacha evam uktvarjunah sankhye rathopastha upavishat visrijya sa-sharam chapam shoka-samvigna-manasah

Sanjay says: Speaking thus, Arjun puts down his bow and arrows, and falls into the seat of his chariot, his mind in confused and burdened with grief.

Chapter 02

sanjaya uvacha tam tatha kripayavishtamashru purnakulekshanam vishidantamidam vakyam uvacha madhusudanah

Sanjay says: Seeing Arjun overwhelmed with sorrow and his eyes full of tears, Shri Krishna spoke, offering Arjun the most precious wisdom of the universe.

shri bhagavan uvacha kutastva kashmalamidam vishame samupasthitam anarya-jushtamaswargyam akirti-karam arjuna

The Lord says: Whence hath this dejection in critical juncture befallen thee, O Arjun? It is unworthy of a good man, heaven-excluding & infamy-bringing.

klaibyam ma sma gamah partha naitat tvayyupapadyate kshudram hridaya-daurbalyam tyaktvottishtha parantapa

To impotence yield not ye, O Pritha's son, It ill-fits thee. Casting this base faint heartiness off, get up, tormentor of foes.

arjuna uvacha katham bhishmam aham sankhye dronam cha madhusudana ishubhih pratiyotsyami pujarhavari-sudana

Arjun says: How in battle, Bhishma & Drona, shall I, O Slayer of Madhu, attack with arrows those who are fit of worshiping, O Slayer of foes?

gurunahatva hi mahanubhavan shreyo bhoktum bhaikshyamapiha loke hatvartha-kamamstu gurunihaiva bhunjiya bhogan rudhira-pradigdhan

Instead of killing these honourable souls, it's better to eat begged food on earth. Wouldn't killing these wealthcraving teachers stain our pleasures with their blood?

na chaitadvidmah kataranno gariyo yadva jayema yadi va no jayeyuh yaneva hatva na jijivishamas te 'vasthitah pramukhe dhartarashtrah

Unclear who is the stronger, Whether we'll win or they'll defeat us. Having slain whom we wouldn't care to live on, are facing us, siding with the sons of Dhritrashtra

karpanya-doshopahata-svabhavah prichchhami tvam dharma-sammudha-chetah yach-chhreyah syannishchitam bruhi tanme shishyaste 'ham shadhi mam tvam prapannam

Arjun admits to Shri Krishna: my warrior dharma is overcome by helplessness. I pray as your disciple, do teach me what is my correct duty.

na hi prapashyami mamapanudyad yach-chhokam uchchhoshanam-indriyanam avapya bhumav-asapatnamriddham rajyam suranamapi chadhipatyam

For I see not, how would it remove my grief, Which withers my senses. Even if I attain the flourishing kingdom of earth, without foes and the lordship of the Shining ones [heavens].

sanjaya uvacha evam-uktva hrishikesham gudakeshah parantapa na yotsya iti govindam uktva tushnim babhuva ha

Sanjay says: Having so spoken to the Lord of senses , The lord of sleep, tormentor of foes. says, "I will not fight," O Govind, and became silent

tam-uvacha hrishikeshah prahasanniva bharata senayorubhayor-madhye vishidantam-idam vachah

O Dhritarashtra, thereafter, in the midst of both armies, Lord of senses [Krishna], as if smiling, says to grief-stricken Arjun.

shri bhagavan uvacha ashochyan-anvashochas-tvam prajna-vadansh cha bhashase gatasun-agatasunsh-cha nanushochanti panditah

The Lord says: For those who deserve no grief thou grievest and words of wisdom thou talkest the wise grieve not over what evolveth and dissolveth ever.

na tvevaham jatu nasam na tvam neme janadhipah na chaiva na bhavishyamah sarve vayamatah param

There never was a time when you, I, and all these kings never existed, nor shall they ever cease to exist hereafter.

dehino 'smin yatha dehe kaumaram yauvanam jara tatha dehantara-praptir dhiras tatra na muhyati

Just as the embodied soul continuously passes from childhood to youth to old age similarly, at the time of death, the soul passes into another body. The wise are not deluded by this.

matra-sparshas tu kaunteya shitoshna-sukha-duhkha-dah agamapayino 'nityas tans-titikshasva bharata

The sensory organs feel, O Kunti's son, the cold, the heat, the pleasure, & the pain these are ever-changing & transient, bear these feelings, 0 scion of Bharat.

yam hi na vyathayantyete purusham purusharshabha sama-duhkha-sukham dhiram so 'mritatvaya kalpate

O Arjun, noblest amongst men, only those who weather these temporary feelings of grief and happiness while maintaining their equilibrium can attain Moksha [liberation from the cycle of birth & death].

nasato vidyate bhavo nabhavo vidyate satah ubhayorapi drishto 'nta stvanayos tattva-darshibhih

The soul is eternal and never ceases to be unlike the body, which is temporary. The seers have observed this truth after studying both.

avinashi tu tadviddhi yena sarvam idam tatam vinasham avyayasyasya na kashchit kartum arhati

The soul is imperishable and no one can destroy it all the bodies in the universe are prevaded by it.

antavanta ime deha nityasyoktah sharirinah anashino 'prameyasya tasmad yudhyasva bharata

Only the body, within which this indestructible soul resides, is perishable. The soul within is eternal, and thus, O Arjun, fight now.

ya enam vetti hantaram yash chainam manyate hatam ubhau tau na vijanito nayam hanti na hanyate

He who views the soul as the slayer & he who treats the soul as slain are both ignorant, for the soul neither slays nor is it slain.

na jayate mriyate va kadachin nayam bhutva bhavita va na bhuyah ajo nityah shashvato 'yam purano na hanyate hanyamane sharire

Soul is neither born, nor does it ever die, never having been, shall never cease to be. The soul is unborn, it is eternal, immortal, and ageless. It is not destroyed when the body is destroyed.

vedavinashinam nityam ya enam ajam avyayam katham sa purushah partha kam ghatayati hanti kam

He who knows this self as imperishable, eternal, unborn, unchanging that person, O Pritha's son, how can he slay or be slain?

vasansi jirnani yatha vihaya navani grihnati naro 'parani tatha sharirani vihaya jirnanya nyani sanyati navani dehi

As a person sheds worn-out garments and wears new ones, likewise, at the time of death, the soul casts off its worn-out body & migrates to a new one.

nainam chhindanti shastrani nainam dahati pavakah na chainam kledayantyapo na shoshayati marutah

Soul cannot be pierced with weapons, nor can be burned by fire, drowned in water, or dissipated by wind.

achchhedyo 'yam adahyo 'yam akledyo 'shoshya eva cha nityah sarva-gatah sthanur achalo 'yam sanatanah

impenetrable, incombustible, un-drownable and indispersable Everlasting, all pervading, firm, unmoving, and ancient is the soul

avyakto 'yam achintyo 'yam avikaryo 'yam uchyate tasmadevam viditvainam nanushochitum arhasi

Without form, beyond comprehension, immutable is the soul. Now you know, therefore you should not grieve.

atha chainam nitya-jatam nityam va manyase mritam tathapi tvam maha-baho naivam shochitum arhasi

Even if you regard the soul to constantly go through the cycle of birth & death, O mighty-armed, you shouldn't grieve.

jatasya hi dhruvo mrityur dhruvam janma mritasya cha tasmad apariharye 'rthe na tvam shochitum arhasi

What is born will certainly die, and rebirth is certain of which dies, So you shouldn't grieve for the inevitable.

avyaktadini bhutani vyakta-madhyani bharata avyakta-nidhananyeva tatra ka paridevana

Unmanifested is the primal state of beings, manifestation is their middle state, and O scion of Bharat, unmanifested again after death, What is there then to grieve?

ashcharya-vat pashyati kashchid enan ashcharya-vad vadati tathaiva chanyah ashcharya-vach chainam anyah shrinoti shrutvapyenam veda na chaiva kashchit

Some regard the soul as marvellous, others marvel to learn about it, and yet some others are unable to understand its marvels, even after hearing about it.

dehi nityam avadhyo 'yam dehe sarvasya bharata tasmat sarvani bhutani na tvam shochitum arhasi

The dweller [soul] is constant, unslayable, and present in everybody, O Bharat, Therefore you shouldn't mourn for anybody

swa-dharmam api chavekshya na vikampitum arhasi dharmyaddhi yuddhach chhreyo 'nyat kshatriyasya na vidyate

As a Kshatriya [warrior], your duty is to fight for and uphold righteousness So do not waver.

yadrichchhaya chopapannam swarga-dvaram apavritam sukhinah kshatriyah partha labhante yuddham idrisham

O Arjun, fortunate are the Kshatriya who are afforded this opportunity. A virtuous battle that grants them passage to Heaven.

atha chet tvam imam dharmyam sangramam na karishyasi tatah sva-dharmam kirtim cha hitva papam avapsyasi

But abandoning this war and rejecting your duty will incur infamy, and sin.

akirtim chapi bhutani kathayishyanti te 'vyayam sambhavitasya chakirtir maranad atirichyate

For a person of your repute and stature, the mark of a deserter and cowardice will be worse than death.

bhayad ranad uparatam mansyante tvam maha-rathah yesham cha tvam bahu-mato bhutva yasyasi laghavam

The great warriors beside whom you have fought will despise you for abandoning a fight and those you fought against will treat you lightly.

avachya-vadansh cha bahun vadishyanti tavahitah nindantastava samarthyam tato duhkhataram nu kim

Belittling you, your honor & your might truly, what could be more painful than that?

hato va prapsyasi swargam jitva va bhokshyase mahim tasmad uttishtha kaunteya yuddhaya krita-nishchayah

If killed in action ascend to Heaven or be victorious & rule this earth Therefore arise, O Kunti's son, to fight with determination.

sukha-duhkhe same kritva labhalabhau jayajayau tato yuddhaya yujyasva naivam papam avapsyasi

Grief or happiness, victory or defeat, remain indifferent to the outcome and fight, thus you shall incur no sin.

esha te 'bhihita sankhye buddhir yoge tvimam shrinu buddhya yukto yaya partha karma-bandham prahasyasi

Thus I've explained to you Gyana Yog, the intellectual perspective of life. Now listen, O Pritha's son, as I explain Karma Yog, with which you can remain free from the bondage of Karmas.

nehabhikrama-nasho 'sti pratyavayo na vidyate svalpam apyasya dharmasya trayate mahato bhayat

Never is this path futile or harmful even a little practice of this Dharma can save the Karmyogi from the terrible fear of death.

vyavasayatmika buddhir ekeha kuru-nandana bahu-shakha hyanantash cha buddhayo 'vyavasayinam

In this [karmyog] there is a singular understanding of resolute determination. However, O Scion of Kuru, for the ignorant, these understandings are many-branched & innumerable.

yamimam pushpitam vacham pravadanty-avipashchitah veda-vada-ratah partha nanyad astiti vadinah kamatmanah swarga-para janma-karma-phala-pradam kriya-vishesha-bahulam bhogaishwarya-gatim prati

In flowery speech indulge the ignorant, taught that the Vedas is final. Their souls are steeped in desire for heaven, and [flowery speech] offers rebirth as the result and prescribes ceremonies manifold for securing wealth & power

bhogaiswvarya-prasaktanam tayapahrita-chetasam vyavasayatmika buddhih samadhau na vidhiyate

In their pursuit of wealth & power the hearts of such devotees are captivated. Not in the understanding of the Divine.

trai-gunya-vishaya veda nistrai-gunyo bhavarjuna nirdvandvo nitya-sattva-stho niryoga-kshema atmavan

Vedas only treat the three traits of Nature [Satva, Rajas, & Tamas], you must grow above these three traits, O Arjun, Free yourself from contradictions [of Happiness & Grief, Success & Failure etc. etc.], ever in thy being rooted, untroubled by acquisition & preservation, & self-controlled.

yavan artha udapane sarvatah samplutodake tavansarveshu vedeshu brahmanasya vijanatah

Of what use is a reservoir in a place which is flooded with water, Of same utility are the Vedas to one who is God-knowing & enlightened.

karmany-evadhikaras te ma phaleshu kadachana ma karma-phala-hetur bhur ma te sango 'stvakarmani

In action alone is your freedom, but never in its results. Act not with a motivation for a return, neither give in to inaction.

yoga-sthah kuru karmani sangam tyaktva dhananjaya siddhy-asiddhyoh samo bhutva samatvam yoga uchyate

Performing actions as per Yoga, abandoning all attachment [of the outcome], O victor of wealth, remaining equanimous in success & failure, this equanimity is called Yoga

durena hy-avaram karma buddhi-yogad dhananjaya buddhau sharanam anvichchha kripanah phala-hetavah

Far inferior are actions taken for [selfish] reasons, O victor of wealth, self-defeating are the ones, who act selfishly.

buddhi-yukto jahatiha ubhe sukrita-dushkrite tasmad yogaya yujyasva yogah karmasu kaushalam

Imbued with poised reason one forsakes good & ill deeds, So strive for this Yoga and become skillful in it.

karma-jam buddhi-yukta hi phalam tyaktva manishinah janma-bandha-vinirmuktah padam gachchhanty-anamayam

Having taken the path of performing selfless actions without an expectation of a reward, Sages freed themselves from endless cycle of rebirth & attained the blissful state.

yada te moha-kalilam buddhir vyatitarishyatitada gantasi nirvedam shrotavyasya shrutasya cha

Only after crossing this mire of delusion your reason will be indifferent to heard [learnt] and to be heard [to be learned]

shruti-vipratipanna te yada sthasyati nishchalasamadhav-achala buddhis tada yogam avapsyasi

Your intellect will cease to be bewildered by any other preachings, for you will already have attained Yoga [enlightenment].

arjuna uvachasthita-prajnasya ka bhasha samadhi-sthasya keshavasthita-dhih kim prabhasheta kim asita vrajeta kim

Arjun asks: O Keshav, what language does such an enlightened one speaks? O Keshav, How does he talk, sit, or walk?

shri bhagavan uvachaprajahati yada kaman sarvan partha mano-gatanatmany-evatmana tushtah sthita-prajnas tadochyate

The Lord replies: When he forsakes cravings ofall worldly desires, and is absolutely content with his own companionship - he is said to be of stable reasoning.

duhkheshv-anudvigna-manah sukheshu vigata-sprihahvita-raga-bhaya-krodhah sthita-dhir munir uchyate

Unperturbed in crisis or immune to elation; free from passion, fear, and anger - He is the stable sage.

yah sarvatranabhisnehas tat tat prapya shubhashubhamnabhinandati na dveshti tasya prajna pratishthita

Unattached in everyway, in whatever he gets, whether fair or foul, Neither rejoices nor bemoans, his understanding becomes stable

yada sanharate chayam kurmo 'nganiva sarvashahindriyanindriyarthebhyas tasya prajna pratishthita

Like a tortoise draws itself into its shell, who withdraws his senses from his sense organs, attains poise.

vishaya vinivartante niraharasya dehinahrasa-varjam raso 'pyasya param drishtva nivartate

Desires recede from the mind of who abstains, so does affection, upon realizing the Truth

yatato hyapi kaunteya purushasya vipashchitahindriyani pramathini haranti prasabham manah

The senses are strong, O Kunti's son, and their pull can sway even the most intelligent and tolerant of men.

tani sarvani sanyamya yukta asita mat-parahvashe hi yasyendriyani tasya prajna pratishthita

Only they can keep their senses under control, who are devoted to Me, Only with disciplined senses, their reason becomes stable.

dhyayato vishayan pumsah sangas teshupajayatesangat sanjayate kamah kamat krodho 'bhijayate

The mind dwells on objects & develops attachments, from attachments, desires are born. These desires [when unfulfilled] turn into anger.

krodhad bhavati sammohah sammohat smriti-vibhramahsmriti-bhranshad buddhi-nasho buddhi-nashat pranashyati

From anger arises delusion, therefrom confusion of memory, from confusion of memory, loss of reason, with reason gone, the man is lost

raga-dvesha-viyuktais tu vishayan indriyaish charanatma-vashyair-vidheyatma prasadam adhigachchhati

By renouncing affection & aversion, senses roam free [of attachments] to objects. With mind being under one's control, man becomes conscious of his pure self and attains tranquility

prasade sarva-duhkhanam hanir asyopajayateprasanna-chetaso hyashu buddhih paryavatishthate

With cessation of all suffering [from detachment], tranquility is born, and with tranquility the reason soon is steadied.

nasti buddhir-ayuktasya na chayuktasya bhavanana chabhavayatah shantir ashantasya kutah sukham

There cannot be stable reasoning without control over senses, without sense control there cannot be meditation, without meditation there cannot be peace, and how can there be happiness without peace?

indriyanam hi charatam yan mano 'nuvidhiyatetadasya harati prajnam vayur navam ivambhasi

Sensual desires can rock a person's intellect like the strong gusts of wind rock an unanchored sail boat and lead it astray.

tasmad yasya maha-baho nigrihitani sarvashahindriyanindriyarthebhyas tasya prajna pratishthita

Therefore, O Mighty Armed, who has completely withdrawn his desires from sense objects, his steadiness is established.

ya nisha sarva-bhutanam tasyam jagarti sanyamiyasyam jagrati bhutani sa nisha pashyato muneh

What seems as night for all beings, the self-controlled keeps awake. In what seems like day for all beings, sleeps the sage who sees.

apuryamanam achala-pratishthamsamudram apah pravishanti yadvattadvat kama yam pravishanti sarvesa shantim apnoti na kama-kami

As ocean remains still even when the gushing rivers steadily pour into it; Likewise desires keep flowing into whom who has attained peace, without affecting him.

vihaya kaman yah sarvan pumansh charati nihsprihahnirmamo nirahankarah sa shantim adhigachchhati

Who gives up desires, no longer competes for proprietorship or ego, lives in peace.

esha brahmi sthitih partha nainam prapya vimuhyati sthitvasyam anta-kale 'pi brahma-nirvanam richchhati

Thus attainting this state of Brahmi [Enlightenment] O Pritha's son, he is no longer deluded. Maintaining this same state till the end [of life] attains Nirvana [Moksh]

Chapter 03

arjuna uvacha jyayasi chet karmanas te mata buddhir janardana tat kim karmani ghore mam niyojayasi keshava

Arjun asks - If reason [knowledge] is superior to action, O Janardan, than why do you prompt me to commit this cruel 'action', O Keshav?

vyamishreneva vakyena buddhim mohayasiva me tad ekam vada nishchitya yena shreyo 'ham apnuyam

Contradictory statements are confusing me, let me know decisively which path is excellent.

shri bhagavan uvacha loke 'smin dvi-vidha nishtha pura prokta mayanagha jnana-yogena sankhyanam karma-yogena yoginam

The Lord says: In this world, the state {of equanimity] by two methods I have indicated before, O sinless, By the Yoga of Knowledge of the Sankhyas And the Yoga of Action of the Yogis.

na karmanam anarambhan naishkarmyam purusho 'shnute na cha sannyasanad eva siddhim samadhigachchhati

Not by abstinence does one remains inactive. Nor by mere renunciation does he attain perfection

na hi kashchit kshanam api jatu tishthatyakarma-krit karyate hyavashah karma sarvah prakriti-jair gunaih

Not for an instant ever can any one rest inactive. Helplessly are all driven to action by the Tri-Gunas [three traits] of Nature

karmendriyani sanyamya ya aste manasa smaran indriyarthan vimudhatma mithyacharah sa uchyate

Their sense organs restrained, yet they dwell on those senses in their mind, such claimants are self-deluded hypocrites.

yas tvindriyani manasa niyamyarabhate 'rjuna karmendriyaih karma-yogam asaktah sa vishishyate

Those who practice self-control & regulate their senses, O Arjun, and perform their actions as per Karmayoga without coercion are superior.

niyatam kuru karma tvam karma jyayo hyakarmanah
sharira-yatrapi cha te na prasiddhyed akarmanah

Perform your duteous actions. Action is superior to inaction. Or if left inactive, this sojourn body will fail.

yajnarthat karmano 'nyatra loko 'yam karma-bandhanah
tad-artham karma kaunteya mukta-sangah samachara

Action not performed as a Yajna [Fire-Ritual], bonds that action-doer to this world. Hence perform your actions, O Kunti's son, as a Yajna & remain bondage-free

saha-yajnah prajah srishtva purovacha prajapatih anena
prasavishyadhvam esha vo 'stvishta-kama-dhuk

With Yajna mankind evolved from the time of creation, The Creator, gave them [Yajna] as the means to prospe & propagate

devan bhavayatanena te deva bhavayantu vah parasparam
bhavayantah shreyah param avapsyatha

The Devas [demi-gods] you serve [through Yajna], the Devas then serve you [through rain] and you both mutually serve the all pervading [God]

ishtan bhogan hi vo deva dasyante yajna-bhavitah tair dattan
apradayaibhyo yo bhunkte stena eva sah

Devas [demi-gods] bestow enjoyments for performing [Yajnas], but those who do not share these enjoyments are in fact thieves.

yajna-shishtashinah santo muchyante sarva-kilbishaih bhunjate te
tvagham papa ye pachantyatma-karanat

Saints enjoy what's left-over after sharing with others & avoid sin, but those who only enjoy everything themselves are sinners.

annad bhavanti bhutani parjanyad anna-sambhavah yajnad bhavati
parjanyo yajnah karma-samudbhavah

Food that sustains all beings, grows because of rains, and rains results from Yajnas - these actions are inter-dependant.

karma brahmodbhavam viddhi brahmakshara-samudbhavam tasmat sarva-gatam brahma nityam yajne pratishthitam

Karmas were created by Brahma and Brahma himself originated from the Almighty, that same all-pervading Almighty is forever present in the Yajna.

evam pravartitam chakram nanuvartayatiha yah aghayur indriyaramo mogham partha sa jivati

The cycle of time keeps turning, the ones who does everything for pleasing their senses, O Pritha's son, they live in vain.

yas tvatma-ratir eva syad atma-triptash cha manavah atmanyeva cha santushtas tasya karyam na vidyate

One rejoicing in the self, illumined in the self Content in the self alone, for they are free from all obligations.

naiva tasya kritenartho nakriteneha kashchana na chasya sarva-bhuteshu kashchid artha-vyapashrayah

Neither without reason he acts or doesn't act, nor he acts for recognition.

tasmad asaktah satatam karyam karma samachara asakto hyacharan karma param apnoti purushah

Therefore always perform all your actions selflessly, only by doing so does one attains the Supreme

karmanaiva hi sansiddhim asthita janakadayah loka-sangraham evapi sampashyan kartum arhasi

King Janak and the likes attained enlightenment by performing actions selflessly for world-harmony, and so can all others who do so.

yad yad acharati shreshthas tat tad evetaro janah sa yat pramanam kurute lokas tad anuvartate

Howsoever the virtuous behave, so does the world follow Whatever standard they set, men unquestioningly follow.

na me parthasti kartavyam trishu lokeshu kinchana nanavaptam avaptavyam varta eva cha karmani

There is nothing that I desire, O Pritha's son, nor anything that I cannot attain effortlessly in all Tri-Lokas [Tri-regions]. Yet, I am engaged in action [Karma]

yadi hyaham na varteyam jatu karmanyatandritah mama vartmanuvartante manushyah partha sarvashah

If I were to not perform any actions [Karmas], everyone everywhere would follow suit, O Pritha's son.

utsideyur ime loka na kuryam karma ched aham sankarasya cha karta syam upahanyam imah prajah

The worlds would perish, if I shun my actions [Karmas] The ensuing confusion would result in total annihilation of all inhabitants.

saktah karmanyavidvanso yatha kurvanti bharata kuryad vidvans tathasaktash chikirshur loka-sangraham

Selfishly act the ignorant, O Bharat, therefore the wise desiring a harmonious world, should act selflessly.

na buddhi-bhedam janayed ajnanam karma-sanginam joshayet sarva-karmani vidvan yuktah samacharan

Without unsettling the ignorant selfish The wise should steadily act to educate them towards selflessness.

prakriteh kriyamanani gunaih karmani sarvashah ahankara-vimudhatma kartaham iti manyate

Depending on the Gunas all Karmas [actions] are performed But blinded by ego, the self thinks himself to be the doer.

tattva-vit tu maha-baho guna-karma-vibhagayoh guna guneshu vartanta iti matva na sajjate

A knower, O Mighty-Armed, knows these divisions of Gunas, hence knows which action is the result of which Guna and not the 'self'.

prakriter guna-sammudhah sajjante guna-karmasu tan akritsna-vido mandan kritsna-vin na vichalayet

Those deluded, act on the basis of their Gunas And lowly acts of such dim-witted perturb themselves.

mayi sarvani karmani sannyasyadhyatma-chetasa nirashir nirmamo bhutva yudhyasva vigata-jvarah

Dedicate all your actions to me with a renunciated mindset, without expectation or ego, shed the fever of doubt and fight.

ye me matam idam nityam anutishthanti manavah shraddhavanto 'nasuyanto muchyante te 'pi karmabhih

Whosoever practices this teaching of mine faithfully, they are undoubtedly liberated from the bondage of Karmas [actions]

ye tvetad abhyasuyanto nanutishthanti me matam sarva-jnana-vimudhans tan viddhi nashtan achetasah

But those who are negligently critical and do not practise this teaching of mine Remain devoid of all true knowledge regard such ignorant folk to be doomed

sadrisham cheshtate svasyah prakriter jnanavan api prakritim yanti bhutani nigrahah kim karishyati

All people act based upon their Gunas [traits of nature], controlled by these Gunas, how can one restraint themselves?

indriyasyendriyasyarthe raga-dveshau vyavasthitau tayor na vasham agachchhet tau hyasya paripanthinau

Senses & their desires inherently imbue passion & anger yield not to them, they are the obstacles of the [righteous] path.

shreyan swa-dharmo vigunah para-dharmat sv-anushthitat swa-dharme nidhanam shreyah para-dharmo bhayavahah

Better is one's self-duty seemingly meritless, than performing another's duty dying in the discharge of one's duty is far better than being proselytized out of fear.

arjuna uvacha atha kena prayukto 'yam papam charati purushah anichchhann api varshneya balad iva niyojitah

Arjun Asks: Then what moves a man to commit sin? Even though unwillingly, O Varshaneya, but as if compelled.

shri bhagavan uvacha kama esha krodha esha rajo-guna-samudbhavah mahashano maha-papma viddhyenam iha vairinam

The Lord replies: It is the craving, it is the anger, due to Rajoguna. All consuming, most sinful, on earth is this enemy [Rajas].

dhumenavriyate vahnir yathadarsho malena cha yatholbenavrito garbhas tatha tenedam avritam

As fire is enveloped by smoke, or mirror by dust, as fetus by membrane, so is this [desire] enveloped by it [Rajoguna]

avritam jnanam etena jnanino nitya-vairina kama-rupena kaunteya dushpurenanalena cha

Knowledge is hidden by this perpetual enemy of the seeker, O Kunti's son, that [enemy] is the insatiable fire of desire.

indriyani mano buddhir asyadhishthanam uchyate etair vimohayatyesha jnanam avritya dehinam

Senses, mind & intelligence are its stations, through these, it [desire] envelopes knowledge & deludes the body-dweller [soul].

tasmat tvam indriyanyadau niyamya bharatarshabha papmanam prajahi hyenam jnana-vijnana-nashanam

So first discipline your senses, O best of Bharats, And slay this [Rajoguna] sinful destroyer of knowledge & wisdom

indriyani paranyahur indriyebhyah param manah manasas tu para buddhir yo buddheh paratas tu sah

Senses are stronger than the body, Mind is stronger than the Senses Intellect is stronger than the mind, but the soul remains far superior.

evam buddheh param buddhva sanstabhyatmanam atmana jahi shatrum maha-baho kama-rupam durasadam

Thus knowing it [Rajoguna] to be stronger than intellect & mind controlling, Slay this enemy [desire], O mighty-armed, as this foe is hard to vanquish

Chapter 04

shri bhagavan uvacha;imam vivasvate yogam proktavan aham avyayam;vivasvan manave praha manur ikshvakave 'bravit

Lord Shri Krishna Says: I taught this Yoga to Viwaswat, Viwaswat taught Manu & Manu taught Ikshwaku

evam parampara-praptam imam rajarshayo viduh;sa kaleneha mahata yogo nashtah parantapa

Thus this knowledge was passed down from generation to generation for eons by the Sage Kings, but with the passage of time it was lost to mankind, O tormentor of foes.

sa evayam maya te 'dya yogah proktah puratanah;bhakto 'si me sakha cheti rahasyam hyetad uttamam

The same ancient Yoga, I am teaching you today, which is the most profound mystery, because you are my devotee & friend.

arjuna uvacha;aparam bhavato janma param janma vivasvatah;katham etad vijaniyam tvam adau proktavan iti

Arjun asks: You were born recently, Viwaswat [Sun] was born at creation, How could have you taught it [to the Sun] at the time of Creation?

shri bhagavan uvacha;bahuni me vyatitani janmani tava charjuna;tanyaham veda sarvani na tvam vettha parantapa

The Lord replied: Many have been my births as well yours, O Arjun, I remember all of them, but you do not, O tormentor of foes.

ajo 'pi sannavyayatma bhutanam ishvaro 'pi san;prakritim svam adhishthaya sambhavamyatma-mayaya

Even though I am unborn, eternal, & Lord of all beings, I manifest my transcendental energy into this form to be discernible by mortal beings.

yada yada hi dharmasya glanir bhavati bharata;abhyutthanam adharmasya tadatmanam srijamyaham

Whenever there is decay of Dharma, O Bharat, And growth of Adharma, I assume a body-form.

paritranaya sadhunam vinashaya cha dushkritam;dharma-sansthapanarthaya sambhavami yuge yuge

For the protection of the good & destruction of the evil-doers. For the re-establishment of true Dharma, I manifest from eons to eons

janma karma cha me divyam evam yo vetti tattvatah;tyaktva deham punar janma naiti mam eti so 'rjuna

My divine birth & its purpose, whosoever comprehends its true essence They upon shedding their body [dying] is not reborn, but comes to me, O Arjun.

vita-raga-bhaya-krodha man-maya mam upashritah;bahavo jnana-tapasa puta mad-bhavam agatah

Freed from attachment, fear and anger, mind absorbed in Me, refuged in Me, Purified in the fire of knowledge, have many attained My Bliss

ye yatha mam prapadyante tans tathaiva bhajamyaham;mama vartmanuvartante manushyah partha sarvashah

In whatever way they pray to me, I accept those who at last tread My path, O Pritha's son, whenever they may commence.

kankshantah karmanam siddhim yajanta iha devatah;kshipram hi manushe loke siddhir bhavati karmaja

Those desiring gratification here [in the mortal realm] serve demigods. Soon they attain such gratifications.

chatur-varnyam maya srishtam guna-karma-vibhagashah;tasya kartaram api mam viddhyakartaram avyayam

Four classes I created based on the division of Guna Karma [Traits of Nature] I created them to be passive & immutable.

na mam karmani limpanti na me karma-phale spriha;iti mam yo 'bhijanati karmabhir na sa badhyate

Neither am I affected by Karmas, nor do I relish its rewards those who know me thus, is not bound by action.

evam jnatva kritam karma purvair api mumukshubhih;kuru karmaiva tasmattvam purvaih purvataram kritam

Thus the learned performed their actions to achieve liberation [You must also] perform actions similarly as they did in the past.

kim karma kim akarmeti kavayo 'pyatra mohitah;tat te karma pravakshyami yaj jnatva mokshyase 'shubhat

What is Karma [action] & what is Akarma [inaction] knowing the difference is puzzling The difference I shall explain, knowing which will save you from inauspicious

karmano hyapi boddhavyam boddhavyam cha vikarmanah;akarmanash cha boddhavyam gahana karmano gatih

It is necessary to know the nature of action, as well as that of forbidden action. Necessary also to know the nature of inaction, mysterious is the path of action.

karmanyakarma yah pashyed akarmani cha karma yah;sa buddhiman manushyeshu sa yuktah kritsna-karma-krit

He who acts when others are inactive, and remains inactive when others react he is wise & expert doer of actions.

yasya sarve samarambhah kama-sankalpa-varjitah;jnanagni-dagdha-karmanam tam ahuh panditam budhah

Whose all commencements [deeds] are without self gratification Tempered in the fires of knowledge, he shall be known as a Pandit.

tyaktva karma-phalasangam nitya-tripto nirashrayah;karmanyabhipravritto 'pi naiva kinchit karoti sah

Who abandons all desire for rewards from his Karmas [actions], remains forever satiated & independent Even when engaged in Karmas [actions], he Who abandons all desire for rewards from his Karmas [actions], remains forever satiated & independent Even when engaged in Karmas [actions], he accures none.

nirashir yata-chittatma tyakta-sarva-parigrahah;shariram kevalam karma kurvan napnoti kilbisham

Hoping for no rewards, with a self controlled mind, without any desires for personal possessions, using the body only for selfless acts, he remains sin free.

yadrichchha-labha-santushto dvandvatito vimatsarah;samah siddhavasiddhau cha kritvapi na nibadhyate

Content with unsought gain, without contradictions equanimous in success or failure, Though acting, he remains unbound [by Karmas]

gata-sangasya muktasya jnanavasthita-chetasah;yajnayacharatah karma samagram praviliyate

Freed from all attachments, established in knowledge When Karmas [Actions] are performed as Yajnas, all activities disintegrate [into aether] like oblations.

brahmarpanam brahma havir brahmagnau brahmana hutam;brahmaiva tena gantavyam brahma-karma-samadhina

Every deed a Yajña, every Karma [action] an oblation, knowledge is the divine fire [of this Yajna], and the presiding deity is me. Those who perform all their Karmas [actions] this way, attain Moksha.

daivam evapare yajnam yoginah paryupasate;brahmagnavapare yajnam yajnenaivopajuhvati

Devas [demigods] are invoked through Yajnas for fulfilling desires, Then there are those who invoke the fire-god to perform Yajnas for Yajna's sake.

shrotradinindriyanyanye sanyamagnishu juhvati;shabdadin vishayananya indriyagnishu juhvati

Others offer their learning etc. in the fire of restraint. Others offer their voice [give-up speaking] etc. in the fire of the senses.

sarvanindriya-karmani   prana-karmani chapare;atma-sanyama-yogagnau juhvati jnana-dipite

Some offer their sensual desires & life actions in the illumined fires of knowledge by becoming a Hermit/Monk [celibate].

dravya-yajnas   tapo-yajna   yoga-yajnas tathapare;swadhyaya-jnana-yajnash cha yatayah sanshita-vratah

Some offer their wealth for helping others, by spreading knowledge and creating means for the betterment of society.

apane juhvati pranam prane 'panam tathapare;pranapana-gati ruddhva pranayama-parayanah;

There are some who practice yogic breathing techniques to control their gunas and awaken their Kundalini

apare niyataharah pranan praneshu juhvati;sarve 'pyete yajna-vido yajna-kshapita-kalmashah

while some fast as a means to control their desires and cleanse their body & sins.

yajna-shishtamrita-bhujo yanti brahma sanatanam;nayam loko 'styayajnasya kuto 'nyah kuru-sattama

Whosoever performs [some form of] Yajna attains the Supreme Eternal. Not the ones who do not, O Best of Kurus.

evam bahu-vidha yajna vitata brahmano mukhe;karma-jan viddhi tan sarvan evam jnatva vimokshyase

Thus are the varieties of Yajnas as uttered by Brahma, performed by different faculties, and they all grant liberation.

shreyan dravya-mayad yajnaj jnana-yajnah parantapa;sarvam karmakhilam partha jnane parisamapyate

Superior to ingredient oblations is the oblation of knowledge, O tormentor of foes, because the entirety of actions, O Pritha's son, culminate in knowledge

tad viddhi pranipatena pariprashnena sevaya;upadekshyanti te jnanam jnaninas tattva-darshinah

Learn this [Yajna] with humility [from a teacher], by enquiry and by service. The learned & the seers of essence will instruct you in this knowledge.

yaj jnatva na punar moham evam yasyasi pandava;yena bhutanyasheshena drakshyasyatmanyatho mayi

Knowing this you will no longer remain deluded O Pandava, By it you will see me present in all beings.

api ched asi papebhyah sarvebhyah papa-krit-tamah;sarvam jnana-plavenaiva vrijinam santarishyasi

Even if you are, of all sinners, the most sinful, with this boat of knowledge you will be able to sail across the sea of sins

yathaidhansi samiddho 'gnir bhasma-sat kurute 'rjuna;jnanagnih sarva-karmani bhasma-sat kurute tatha

As the fuel is burnt by the fire, O Arjun, similarly Karmas [actions] are burnt away in the fire of knowledge.

na hi jnanena sadrisham pavitramiha vidyate;tatsvayam yogasansiddhah kalenatmani vindati

Nothing purer than knowledge is known, for achieving perfection in Yoga, achieved in due time from within the Self.

shraddhavanllabhate jnanam tat-parah sanyatendriyah;jnanam labdhva param shantim achirenadhigachchhati

Faithfuls discipline their senses & speedily gain knowledge With knowledge gained, they easily attain supreme peace.

ajnash chashraddadhanash cha sanshayatma vinashyati;nayam loko 'sti na paro na sukham sanshayatmanah

The ignorant, devoid of faith & torn with self doubt, perish. There is no happiness for them, neither in this world nor the next.

yoga-sannyasta-karmanam jnana-sanchhinna-sanshayam;atmavantam na karmani nibadhnanti dhananjaya

Who has renounced [selfish actions] Karmas like a Sanyasi [hermit] & torn asunder the veil of doubt Such self-controlled is not bound by Karmas [actions], O Winner of Wealth.

tasmad ajnana-sambhutam hrit-stham jnanasinatmanah;chhittvainam sanshayam yogam atishthottishtha bharata

Hence the doubt born & residing in your heart must be slain with this knowledge of the Self slash that doubt, steady in Yoga, rise up O Bharat.

Chapter 05

arjuna uvacha sannyasam karmanam krishna punar yogam cha shansasi yach chhreya etayor ekam tan me bruhi su-nishchitam

Arjun says: You have praised both Sanyas [renunciation], O Krishna, as well as the path of Karma [selfless actions] Of the two, which one is better, tell me decisively.

shri bhagavan uvacha sannyasah karma-yogash cha nihshreyasa-karavubhau tayos tu karma-sannyasat karma-yogo vishishyate

The Lord replies: Sanyas [Renunciation] & Karma Yoga [Yoga of Action] both lead to the highest good But of the two, Karma Yoga is indeed better than Sanyas.

jneyah sa nitya-sannyasi yo na dveshti na kankshati nirdvandvo hi maha-baho sukham bandhat pramuchyate

Know him to be a Sannyasi, who neither dislikes nor craves, Free from contradictions, Oh mighty armed, such a one is easily released from bondage

sankhya-yogau prithag balah pravadanti na panditah ekamapyasthitah samyag ubhayor vindate phalam

Sankhya & [Karma] Yoga being different is talked by the immature, not by the learned One fully devoted to either path reaps the same fruit.

yat sankhyaih prapyate sthanam tad yogair api gamyate ekam sankhyam cha yogam cha yah pashyati sa pashyati

Stature gained by Sankhyas [Sanyasis], the same is gained by the Yogis [Karma Yogis] Sankhya & Yoga are the same, only those who realize this fact, know the truth.

sannyasas tu maha-baho duhkham aptum ayogatah yoga-yukto munir brahma na chirenadhigachchhati

Attainment of Sanyas [Renunciation], O mighty armed, is harder for the untrained While a [Karma] Yogi sage reaches the Supreme earlier [than Sanyasis].

yoga-yukto vishuddhatma vijitatma jitendriyah sarva-bhutatma-bhutatma kurvann api na lipyate

An Enriched [Karma] Yogi, Purified Soul, Victorious Soul, Conqueror of Senses Viewing all embodied as the primeval spirit, his actions remain untainted

naiva kinchit karomiti yukto manyeta tattva-vit pashyan shrinvan sprishanjighrann ashnangachchhan svapanshvasan

A [Sanyasi] considers himself being actionless, even though, he sees, hears, touches, smells, eats, moves, sleeps, breathes [continued in the next shlok]

pralapan visrijan grihnann unmishan nimishann api indriyanindriyartheshu vartanta iti dharayan

Speaks, gives, receives, blinks All these functions of the senses are considered Karmas [actions]

brahmanyadhaya karmani sangam tyaktva karoti yah lipyate na sa papena padma-patram ivambhasa

Dedicating Karmas [actions] to the Supreme, who acts without expecting a reward. He remains untouched by sin like water droplet on a lotus-leaf

kayena manasa buddhya kevalair indriyair api yoginah karma kurvanti sangam tyaktvatma-shuddhaye

Through body, mind, intellect and senses, Yogis act without expectation for any reward, but only for self-purification.

yuktah karma-phalam tyaktva shantim apnoti naishthikim ayuktah kama-karena phale sakto nibadhyate

Enriched, renunciating expectation of a reward, he [Yogi] attains enduring peace Those lacking [in Yoga], pursue selfish goals, are bound [to this mortal realm].

sarva-karmani manasa sannyasyaste sukham vashi nava-dvare pure dehi naiva kurvan na karayan

All Karmas of renounced, mind lives happily In this nine-gated city [body], free from thinking themselves as the doers or the cause of anything

na kartritvam na karmani lokasya srijati prabhuh na karma-phala-sanyogam svabhavas tu pravartate

Neither agency nor activity [of Karmas] is created by God Neither the results of such Karmas, they are inherent in the nature [of the doer].

nadatte kasyachit papam na chaiva sukritam vibhuh ajnanenavritam jnanam tena muhyanti jantavah

The Lord is never involved in any beings sinful or virtuous deeds It's ignorance that envelopes wisdom, thereby deluding creatures.

jnanena tu tad ajnanam yesham nashitam atmanah tesham aditya-vaj jnanam prakashayati tat param

Whose ignorance is destroyed by knowledge of the self For them knowledge, like the sun illumines the Supreme

tad-buddhayas tad-atmanas tan-nishthas tat-parayanah gachchhantyapunar-avrittim jnana-nirdhuta-kalmashah

Reason abiding in that [God], mind absorbed in that [God], rooted in that [God], devoted to that [God] They leave [this mortal realm] never to return, as their sins are washed away by knowledge.

vidya-vinaya-sampanne brahmane gavi hastini shuni chaiva shva-pake cha panditah sama-darshinah

To a humble learned Brahman, a cow, an elephant, a dog and a dog-eater Are all considered equal.

ihaiva tair jitah sargo yesham samye sthitam manah nirdosham hi samam brahma tasmad brahmani te sthitah

Even here in this mortal realm they gain [happiness], whose minds are equanimous Because the Supreme is flawless, as are those [equanimous] established in it.

na prahrishyet priyam prapya nodvijet prapya chapriyam sthira-buddhir asammudho brahma-vid brahmani sthitah

Neither rejoices on obtaining pleasantness nor grieves on obtaining the unpleasantness [Yogi's] Reason remains steadfast & clear minded for being established in the Divine.

bahya-sparsheshvasaktatma vindatyatmani yat sukham sa brahma-yoga-yuktatma sukham akshayam ashnute

Whose Self is unaffected by external stimuli finds happiness within Such God unioned Self enjoys bliss unending

ye hi sansparsha-ja bhoga duhkha-yonaya eva te adyantavantah kaunteya na teshu ramate budhah

These [external stimuli] enjoyments are verily wombs of pain As they are fleetingly transient, O Son of Kunti, the knower is not swayed by them.

shaknotihaiva yah sodhum prak sharira-vimokshanat kama-krodhodbhavam vegam sa yuktah sa sukhi narah

One who is able to withstand [external stimuli] on earth before casting off his body, The surges that are produced by craving & anger, he's enriched & a happy man

yo 'ntah-sukho 'ntar-aramas tathantar-jyotir eva yah sa yogi brahma-nirvanam brahma-bhuto 'dhigachchhati

He who is joyous within, who enjoys within, whois illumined within; That Yogi finds Moksh and merges with the Brahman.

labhante brahma-nirvanam rishayah kshina-kalmashah chhinna-dvaidha yatatmanah sarva-bhuta-hite ratah

Yogis enjoy divine communion having their sins worn away, Dualities torn asunder, they are self-restrained and intent on welfare of all

kama-krodha-viyuktanam yatinam yata-chetasam abhito brahma-nirvanam vartate viditatmanam

Free of desire and anger, devotees, mind under control, Divine communion lies at hand to the knowers of Self sparshan kritva bahir bahyansh chakshush chaivantare bhruvoh pranapanau samau kritva nasabhyantara-charinau

Keeping external stimuli out, with eyes fixed amidst the eyebrows equalizing inhalation & exhalation.

yatendriya-mano-buddhir munir moksha-parayanah vigatechchha-bhaya-krodho yah sada mukta eva sah

Controlling the senses, mind and reason, a sage intent on liberation, he who lives renouncing desire and free of anger is indeed liberated

bhoktaram yajna-tapasam sarva-loka-maheshvaram suhridam sarva-bhutanam jnatva mam shantim richchhati

Enjoyer of all sacrifices & austerities and Lord of all the realms, And comrade of all beings, having known Me so, he [Yogi] attains peace.

Chapter 06

shri bhagavan uvacha anashritah karma-phalam karyam karma karoti yah sa sannyasi cha yogi cha na niragnir na chakriyah

The Lord says: Those who abandon any expectation from their obligatory duties, is a Sanyasi as well as a Yogi, not the one who abandons Yajna or Worldly chores.

yam sannyasam iti prahur yogam tam viddhi pandava na hyasannyasta-sankalpo yogi bhavati kashchana

That which is called Sanyas [renunciation] is also [Karma] Yoga, O Pandava, because without renunciation how can one become a Yogi?

arurukshor muner yogam karma karanam uchyate yogarudhasya tasyaiva shamah karanam uchyate

Aspiring sages reason Karma [actions] to be the means [of achieving Yoga]; Those established in Yoga, reason tranquility [meditation] to be the means [of achieving Yoga].

yada hi nendriyartheshu na karmasv-anushajjate sarva-sankalpa-sannyasi yogarudhas tadochyate

When neither for the sake of sensual pleasures nor for rewards for his Karmas [actions]; Renouncing all desires, does one establish himself in Yoga.

uddhared atmanatmanam natmanam avasadayet atmaiva hyatmano bandhur atmaiva ripur atmanah

Elevate yourself in your own eyes, don't let your self-esteem fall; Verily you are your own best friend & your own worst enemy.

bandhur atmatmanas tasya yenatmaivatmana jitah anatmanas tu shatrutve vartetatmaiva shatru-vat

He is a friend of himself when one can control himself; Uncontrollable self becomes a hostile enemy.

jitatmanah prashantasya paramatma samahitah shitoshna-sukha-duhkheshu tatha manapamanayoh

A self-controlled [person] dedicated to God becomes serene & equiposed; In cold or heat, joy or sorrow, fame or infamy.

jnana-vijnana-triptatma kuta-stho vijitendriyah yukta ityuchyate yogi sama-loshtashma-kanchanah

Satiated with knowledge & self realization, unpertubed and self-controlled; Yukt [enriched] is such Yogi called, to him clay, stone, or gold are all worth the same.

suhrin-mitraryudasina-madhyastha-dveshya-bandhushu sadhushvapi cha papeshu sama-buddhir vishishyate

Who adopts same attitude towards well-wishers, friends, foes, neutrals, and arbiters, the jealous and relatives. Even towards the pious & the sinners, he is better still.

yogi yunjita satatam atmanam rahasi sthitah ekaki yata-chittatma nirashir aparigrahah

A Yogi should meditate regularly, concentrating while seated in a quiet place. Alone, with mind and self controlled, without expectation and [sense of] possession.

shuchau deshe pratishthapya sthiram asanam atmanah natyuchchhritam nati-nicham chailajina-kushottaram

[Meditate] In a pure [clean] spot having prepared a firm seat. Neither too high nor too low with Kusa grass, deer-skin and cloth.

tatraikagram manah kritva yata-chittendriya-kriyah upavishyasane yunjyad yogam atma-vishuddhaye

Concentrating & keeping in check the activities of the senses & the mind, Sitting on his seat he [aspirant Yogi] should practise Yoga [meditate] for self-purity.

samam kaya-shiro-grivam dharayann achalam sthirah samprekshya nasikagram svam dishash chanavalokayan

Holding the body, head & neck, unmoved & straight; Gazing at tip of the nose without glancing elsewhere.

prashantatma vigata-bhir brahmachari-vrate sthitah manah sanyamya mach-chitto yukta asita mat-parah

Remain serene, fearless, and continent; Concentrating & meditating [my name] and devoted to Me.

yunjann evam sadatmanam yogi niyata-manasah shantim nirvana-paramam mat-sanstham adhigachchhati

With regular meditations a Yogi's mind is disciplined; Serene and unattached, [the Yogi] finds communion with my Divine Bliss

natyashnatastu yogo 'sti na chaikantam anashnatah na chati-svapna-shilasya jagrato naiva charjuna

Yoga is not for the over-eater, nor the under-eater, Nor for one who over-sleeps or under-sleeps, O Arjun.

yuktahara-viharasya yukta-cheshtasya karmasu yukta-svapnavabodhasya yogo bhavati duhkha-ha

Equilibrium in eating & recreation, working, sleeping, & waking; Such Yogi's sorrows are destroyed.

yada viniyatam chittam atmanyevavatishthate nihsprihah sarva-kamebhyo yukta ityuchyate tada

When the disciplined mind abides solely in the self. Man freed from yearning in all objects of desire, is then known as "Yukt" [Enriched].

yatha dipo nivata-stho nengate sopama smrita yogino yata-chittasya yunjato yogam atmanah

As a lamp remains flicker-free in a windless place, so does the thoughts of a displined Yogi do not wander.

yatroparamate chittam niruddham yoga-sevaya yatra chaivatmanatmanam pashyann atmani tushyati

When the inner joy is found [with meditation] and the mind becomes restrained through Yoga; Then the Self realizes the soul and remains satisfied.

sukham atyantikam yat tad buddhi-grahyam atindriyam vetti yatra na chaivayam sthitash chalati tattvatah

Thus the utmost happiness is found by transcending beyond senses; Upon realization, he [Yogi] never forgets the Eternal Truth.

yam labdhva chaparam labham manyate nadhikam tatah yasmin sthito na duhkhena gurunapi vichalyate

Having gained that [Self Realization], no other gain seems greater; Established therein [in Self Realization] not any overwhelming sorrow can perturb him [Yogi].

tam vidyad duhkha-sanyoga-viyogam yogasanjnitam sa nishchayena yoktavyo yogo 'nirvinna-chetasa

Understand that the state of severing ties with unhappiness is known as Yoga; therefore it [Yoga] should be practised with a relentless determination.

sankalpa-prabhavan kamans tyaktva sarvan asheshatah manasaivendriya-gramam viniyamya samantatah

Resolutely & completely forsaking every desire born in the mind; And with every sense organ restrained [contd. in the next verse]

shanaih shanair uparamed buddhya dhriti-grihitaya atma-sanstham manah kritva na kinchid api chintayet

Slowly, steadily, and patiently he [Yogi's] should guide his intellect to stop worrying mindlessly.

yato yato nishcharati manash chanchalam asthiram tatas tato niyamyaitad atmanyeva vasham nayet

Whenever the restless & unsteady mind wanders [into worrying]. [The Yogi should practice] to bring the mind back under Self's control.

prashanta-manasam hyenam yoginam sukham uttamam upaiti shanta-rajasam brahma-bhutam akalmasham

Peaceful and calmed mind grants greatest happiness to the Yogi; With such calmness comes sinfree God Realization.

yunjann evam sadatmanam yogi vigata-kalmashah sukhena brahma-sansparsham atyantam sukham ashnute

Thus trained mind of a Yogi always remains sin-free; Easily connects with Divinity & attains highest bliss.

sarva-bhuta-stham atmanam sarva-bhutani chatmani ikshate yoga-yuktatma sarvatra sama-darshanah

Every living being's soul is a part of the same primeval soul that lies within himself; Hence the Yoga enriched soul considers every living being the same.

yo mam pashyati sarvatra sarvam cha mayi pashyati tasyaham na pranashyami sa cha me na pranashyati

Therefore who sees Me in every living being and every living being in Me, I am always visible to him & as he is to me.

sarva-bhuta-sthitam yo mam bhajatyekatvam asthitah sarvatha vartamano 'pi sa yogi mayi vartate

Whoever realizes the oneness of everything & worships Me, as being present in each & every living being, no matter what he does - such a Yogi is always with and present in me.

atmaupamyena sarvatra samam pashyati yo 'rjuna sukham va yadi va duhkham sa yogi paramo matah

When one beings to realize, as he would his own, O Arjuna, every other living being's happiness or sorrow, that Yogi is the greatest.

arjuna uvacha yo 'yam yogas tvaya proktah samyena madhusudana etasyaham na pashyami chanchalatvat sthitim sthiram

Arjun Says: - The Yoga of Equanimity described by you, O Madhusoodna, I do not see a enduring continauce of it due to the restlessness [of the mind].

chanchalam hi manah krishna pramathi balavad dridham tasyaham nigraham manye vayor iva su-dushkaram

The restless mind, O Krishna, is impetuous, powerful & obstinate; Controlling the mind is like grasping the wind unsuccessfully.

shri bhagavan uvacha asanshayam maha-baho mano durnigraham chalam abhyasena tu kaunteya vairagyena cha grihyate

The Lord Replies: Undoubtedly, O Mighty-Armed, restless mind is hard to restraint; O Kunti's son, but with practice and renunciation it can be subdued.

asanyatatmana yogo dushprapa iti me matih vashyatmana tu yatata shakyo 'vaptum upayatah

It is difficult to control the mind for someone untrained in Yoga; But for someone who is trained [in Yoga] it is indeed possible.

arjuna uvacha ayatih shraddhayopeto yogach chalita-manasah aprapya yoga-sansiddhim kan gatim krishna gachchhati

Arjun Asks: Failed devoted aspirants, who practice Yoga, but are distracted before achieving perfection, what happens to such aspirants, O Krishna?

kachchin nobhaya-vibhrashtash chhinnabhram iva nashyati apratishtho maha-baho vimudho brahmanah pathi

Will [aspirants] wandered from either paths [of Yoga], dissipate like clouds? Did unestablished [aspirants], O Mighty-Armed, vainly tried, only to lose the Eternal path.

etan me sanshayam krishna chhettum arhasyasheshatah tvad-anyah sanshayasyasya chhetta na hyupapadyate

This doubt of mine, O Krishna, only you are fit to destroy completely; None other remover of this doubt as capable as you can be found.

shri bhagavan uvacha partha naiveha namutra vinashas tasya vidyate na hi kalyana-krit kashchid durgatim tata gachchhati

The Lord Replies: Pritha's son, neither here [in the mortal realm] nor in the after world is he [aspirant] destroyed. My dear friend, the practitioner of auspicious [Yoga] never falls to the lower realms.

prapya punya-kritam lokan ushitva shashvatih samah shuchinam shrimatam gehe yoga-bhrashto 'bhijayate

Reaching higher realms, the righteous [aspirants], enjoy for long periods; Then in pure & prosperous home, the failed aspirant, is reborn.

atha va yoginam eva kule bhavati dhimatam etad dhi durlabhataram loke janma yad idrisham

Or in the family of the wise Yogis he [failed aspirant] is reborn; But very rare in this mortal realm is a birth of this kind.

tatra tam buddhi-sanyogam labhate paurva-dehikam yatate cha tato bhuyah sansiddhau kuru-nandana

There his wisdom, from his previous birth, is rekindled; He then continues his journey towards attaining Yoga, O Scion of Kuru.

purvabhyasena tenaiva hriyate hyavasho 'pi sah jijnasur api yogasya shabda-brahmativartate

Pre-Practiced [in the previous birth] he [failed aspirant] is involuntarily inquisitive [about Yoga]; And this curiosity [leads him to] transcend the Vedic ritualism.

prayatnad yatamanas tu yogi sanshuddha-kilbishah aneka-janma-sansiddhas tato yati param gatim

Striving in spirituality the Yogi is cleansed of his sins; Perfected [in Yoga] after many rebirths, he finally reaches the ultimate destination.

tapasvibhyo 'dhiko yogi jnanibhyo 'pi mato 'dhikah karmibhyash chadhiko yogi tasmad yogi bhavarjuna

A Yogi is superior than an ascetic, even superior than the knower of scriptures; And certainly superior than one who acts [selfishly], therefore become a Yogi, O Arjun.

yoginam api sarvesham mad-gatenantar-atmana shraddhavan bhajate yo mam sa me yuktatamo matah

And amongst the Yogis, those devoted in Me; Who faithfully worships Me, I regard him the best enriched [in Yoga].

Chapter 07

śhrī bhagavān uvācha| mayyāsakta-manāḥ pārtha yogaṁ yuñjan mad-āśhrayaḥ| asanśhayaṁ samagraṁ māṁ yathā jñāsyasi tach chhṛiṇu

The Lord Says: Mind devoted to Me, O Pritha's son, depending on Me, practicing Yoga; Undoubtedly merges with me, listen to know how.

jñānam te 'ham sa-vijñānam idaṁ vakṣhyāmyaśheṣhataḥ| yaj jñātvā neha bhūyo 'nyaj jñātavyam-avaśhiṣhyate

That knowledge & wisdom I shall impart in its entirety; Knowing which, there is nothing more in this world, that remains worthy of knowing.

manuṣhyāṇāṁ sahasreṣhu kaśhchid yatati siddhaye| yatatām api siddhānāṁ kaśhchin māṁ vetti tattvataḥ

Amongst thousands of men, only a few strive for perfection [in Yoga]; Even Amongst them, very few know my true essence.

bhūmir-āpo 'nalo vāyuḥ khaṁ mano buddhir eva cha| ahankāra itīyaṁ me bhinnā prakṛitir aṣhṭadhā

Earth, water, fire, air, ether, mind, intellect, And egoism, these are the eight characteristics of the nature I created.

apareyam itas tvanyāṁ prakṛitiṁ viddhi me parām| jīva-bhūtāṁ mahā-bāho yayedaṁ dhāryate jagat

Apart from these lesser qualities of my primal nature; There is the life-force, O Mighty-armed, which sustains this universe.

etad-yonīni bhūtāni sarvāṇītyupadhāraya| ahaṁ kṛitsnasya jagataḥ prabhavaḥ pralayas tathā

These are the two wombs of all manifested living beings; Originate from Me & dissolve in Me at the end.

mattaḥ parataraṁ nānyat kiñchid asti dhanañjaya| mayi sarvam idaṁ protaṁ sūtre maṇi-gaṇā iva

Beyond Me there is nothing whatsoever, O Victor of Wealth. Everything is threaded in Me, like beads on a string.

raso 'ham apsu kaunteya prabhāsmi śhaśhi-sūryayoḥ| praṇavaḥ sarva-vedeṣhu śhabdaḥ khe pauruṣham nṛiṣhu

I am sapidity in water, O Kunti's Son, the light in the sun & the moon; The OM [AUM] in all Vedas, sound in ether [Akash], manhood in men.

puṇyo gandhaḥ pṛithivyām cha tejaśh chāsmi vibhāvasau| jīvanam sarva-bhūteṣhu tapaśh chāsmi tapasviṣhu

[I am] Pious fragrance in earth, glow in fire; Life in all beings, and austerities of the ascetics.

bījam mām sarva-bhūtānām viddhi pārtha sanātanam| buddhir buddhimatām asmi tejas tejasvinām aham

Know Me to be the eternal seed of every living being, O Pritha's son; I am the reason of the wise, and radiance of the illustrious.

balam balavatām chāham kāma-rāga-vivarjitam| dharmāviruddho bhūteṣhu kāmo 'smi bharatarṣhabha

I am the strength of the strong who are devoid of selfish interests and desires; The desire in all livings beings that conforms with Dharma, O Bull of Bharats.

ye chaiva sāttvikā bhāvā rājasās tāmasāśh cha ye| matta eveti tān viddhi na tvaham teṣhu te mayi

And these Satvic, Rajasic, and Tamsic states of existence; Know them from Me, yet I am not in them nor they in me.

tribhir guṇa-mayair bhāvair ebhiḥ sarvam idam jagat| mohitam nābhijānāti māmebhyaḥ param avyayam

These three traits [Satva, Rajas, Tamas] delude this whole world; Mesmerised [by these traits, the world remains] unaware of the imperishable primeval Me.

daivī hyeṣhā guṇa-mayī mama māyā duratyayā| mām eva ye prapadyante māyām etām taranti te

My divinity is veiled by Maya of these three traits [Satva, Rajas, Tamas] and difficult to cross; Only those devoted to Me are able to get through.

na māṁ duṣhkṛitino mūḍhāḥ prapadyante narādhamāḥ|
māyayāpahṛita-jñānā āsuraṁ bhāvam āśhritāḥ

Undevout to Me are the sinners, ignorant, and the vile men; Deprived of knowledge due to Maya, having demonic disposition.

chatur-vidhā bhajante māṁ janāḥ sukṛitino 'rjuna| ārto jijñāsur arthārthī jñānī cha bharataṛṣhabha

Four types of pious people worship Me, O Arjun. The distressed [due to sickness or tragedy], the inquisitive, the wealth seeker, and the knowledgeable devotee, O Bull of Bharats.

teṣhāṁ jñānī nitya-yukta eka-bhaktir viśhiṣhyate| priyo hi jñānino 'tyartham ahaṁ sa cha mama priyaḥ

Of these [4 pious worshippers], especially the knowledgable is forever immersed and solely devoted to Me; To him I am dearest and he is dearest to Me.

udārāḥ sarva evaite jñānī tvātmaiva me matam| āsthitaḥ sa hi yuktātmā mām evānuttamāṁ gatim

Noble they all are [4 pious worshippers], but the knowledgable should be treated as My very Self; Because he is completely immersed in Me, he only seeks divine communion [Moksh].

bahūnāṁ janmanām ante jñānavān māṁ prapadyate| vāsudevaḥ sarvam iti sa mahātmā su-durlabhaḥ

After many rebirths, such knowledgable [devotee] merges with Me; Realizing that it is Me [Vasudev] everywhere, such great soul is indeed very rare.

kāmais tais tair hṛita-jñānāḥ prapadyante 'nya-devatāḥ| taṁ taṁ niyamam āsthāya prakṛityā niyatāḥ svayā

Those whose knowledge is enveloped by cravings, worship Demigods; Performing various rituals driven by their wants.

yo yo yāṁ yāṁ tanuṁ bhaktaḥ śhraddhayārchitum ichchhati|
tasya tasyāchalāṁ śhraddhāṁ tām eva vidadhāmyaham

In whichever form [a Demigod] is worshipped for recieving [a
reward]; I steady that devotee's faith in that form.

sa tayā śhraddhayā yuktas tasyārādhanam īhate| labhate cha tataḥ
kāmān mayaiva vihitān hi tān

The worshipper invokes that Demigod with his faith; Whatever
desires he wished for are in fact granted by Me.

antavat tu phalaṁ teṣhāṁ tad bhavatyalpa-medhasām| devān
deva-yajo yānti mad-bhaktā yānti mām api

Perishable are their [worshipper's] gifts, whose understanding is
limited; Such worshippers only reach the Demigods, whereas my
worshippers reach Me.

avyaktaṁ vyaktim āpannaṁ manyante mām abuddhayaḥ| paraṁ
bhāvam ajānanto mamāvyayam anuttamam

[I am] Indiscernable, but discernable the unwise believe Me to be;
Ignorant of My supreme, limitless, & exalted form.

nāhaṁ prakāśhaḥ sarvasya yoga-māyā-samāvṛitaḥ| mūḍho 'yaṁ
nābhijānāti loko mām ajam avyayam

Enveloped by My Yoga-Maya I am remain invisible to everybody;
The deluded in this world do not know Me as the unborn & limitless.

vedāhaṁ samatītāni vartamānāni chārjuna| bhaviṣhyāṇi cha
bhūtāni māṁ tu veda na kaśhchana

I am aware of beings gone in the past, here in the present, O Arjun;
And of those who will come in the future, but none know about Me.

ichchhā-dveṣha-samutthena dvandva-mohena bhārata|
sarva-bhūtāni sammohaṁ sarge yānti parantapa

Torn between the contradictions of desires & aversions, O Bharat;
All beings are mesmerized upon entering [this mortal realm], O
tormentor of Enemies.

yeṣhāṁ tvanta-gataṁ pāpaṁ janānāṁ puṇya-karmaṇām| te
dvandva-moha-nirmuktā bhajante mām dṛiḍha-vratāḥ

Those people whose sins have been erased due to their righteous deeds; Freed from the contradictions [of desires & aversions], they worship Me devotedly.

jarā-maraṇa-mokṣhāya mām āśhritya yatanti ye| te brahma tadviduḥ kṛitsnam adhyātmaṁ karma chākhilam

[They] find liberation [Moksh] from aging & dying, those devoted in Me; Realizing the Brahman through spirituality & righteous deeds.

sādhibhūtādhidaivaṁ mām sādhiyajñaṁ cha ye viduḥ| prayāṇa-kāle 'pi cha māṁ te vidur yukta-chetasaḥ

They realize that I am the Primeval Matter, Primeval Celestial, and the Primeval Yajna [fire ritual]; Even at the time of their departure [from this mortal realm], they remember [the above mentioned fact] about Me.

Chapter 08

arjuna uvacha kim tad brahma kim adhyatmam kim karma purushottama adhibhutam cha kim proktam adhidaivam kim uchyate

Arjun Asks: What is that Brahman, what is Adhyatma and what is Karma, O Purushottam? What is Adhibhut and Adhidaiva, why are they called so?

adhiyajnah katham ko 'tra dehe 'smin madhusudana prayana-kale cha katham jneyo 'si niyatatmabhih

Arjun Asks: Who and what is Adhiyajna in this body, O Slayer of Madhu? At the time of departure [from this mortal realm], tell me how are You remembered by the knowlegable?

shri bhagavan uvacha aksharam brahma paramam svabhavo 'dhyatmam uchyate bhuta-bhavodbhava-karo visargah karma-sanjnitah

Lord replies: The Imperishable Supreme is Brahma. The intrinsic nature [conscience] is Adhyatma. The interaction of a being, depending upon his conscience, with the nature [& other living beings] on the whole is the Karma.

adhibhutam ksharo bhavah purushash chadhidaivatam adhiyajno 'ham evatra dehe deha-bhritam vara

Adhibhut is the perishable union of Primeval Materials personifying the Primeval being Adhidaiva. The Adhiyajna is the Primeval life-force residing in that embodied being.

anta-kale cha mam eva smaran muktva kalevaram yah prayati sa mad-bhavam yati nastyatra sanshayah

In the end, those who are leaving [this mortal realm], and had meditated on Me [while alive]; Such departing [souls], without doubt, merge with Me.

yam yam vapi smaran bhavam tyajatyante kalevaram tam tam evaiti kaunteya sada tad-bhava-bhavitah

Or whomsoever one meditated about while alive; After being reincarnated, O Kunti's son, they will achieve them.

tasmat sarveshu kaleshu mam anusmara yudhya cha mayyarpita-mano-buddhir mam evaishyasyasanshayam

Therefore remember Me at all times and also while fighting; Surrender your mind & reason to Me, you will certainly attain Me.

abhyasa-yoga-yuktena chetasa nanya-gamina paramam purusham divyam yati parthanuchintayan

An unwandering & Yoga enriched practiced intellect; Dedicated to the Supreme Divine Being, O Pritha's son, he goes to Him.

kavim puranam anushasitaram anor aniyansam anusmared yah sarvasya dhataram achintya-rupam aditya-varnam tamasah parastat

The All-knowing, Ancient, Sovereign, Subtler than the Subtlest, Whoever meditates upon [him]; The Sustainer of all, Inconceivable form, Brighter than the Sun, beyond all Darkness;

prayana-kale manasachalena bhaktya yukto yoga-balena chaiva bhruvor madhye pranam aveshya samyak sa tam param purusham upaiti divyam

At the time of departing [from this mortal realm], dedicated in devotion through Yoga's strength; Concentrating their life-force between their eye-brows, he merges with the Supreme Divine Being.

yad aksharam veda-vido vadanti vishanti yad yatayo vita-ragah yad ichchhanto brahmacharyam charanti tat te padam sangrahena pravakshye

Whom the Vedic scholars call the Imperishable, whom the ascetics seek by remaining celibate, that Goal I shall describe briefly.

sarva-dvarani sanyamya mano hridi nirudhya cha murdhnyadhayatmanah pranam asthito yoga-dharanam

Restraining all the gates [of the body: Ears, Eyes, Nostrils, Mouth, Anus and Genitals], concentrating the mind in the heart [Chest region]; Drawing the life-force through the forehead, in a Yogic state.

om ityekaksharam brahma vyaharan mam anusmaran yah prayati tyajan deham sa yati paramam gatim

Chanting the Monosyllable OM [AUM], remembering Me as the Brahman; Departs from his body, he attains the Divine Path [merges with Me].

ananya-chetah satatam yo mam smarati nityashah tasyaham sulabhah partha nitya-yuktasya yoginah

With unswerving mind who always meditates on Me; For such Yogis it is easy, O Pritha's son, to always attain Me.

mam upetya punar janma duhkhalayam ashashvatam napnuvanti mahatmanah sansiddhim paramam gatah

Having attained Me, [Yogis] are freed from cycle of rebirth and this mortal realm of sorrows; Great souls, who have achieved perfection [through Yoga] never suffer.

a-brahma-bhuvanal lokah punar avartino 'rjuna mam upetya tu kaunteya punar janma na vidyate

Until reaching the Realm of Brahma, beings [of all realms] go through rebirth, O Arjun; But after reaching Me, O Kunti's Son, one is freed from rebirth.

sahasra-yuga-paryantam ahar yad brahmano viduh ratrim yuga-sahasrantam te 'ho-ratra-vido janah

A Day of Brahma lasts a thousand Yugas; And Brahma's Night lasts another thousand Yugas, this [period of Day & Night] is known to the wise.

avyaktad vyaktayah sarvah prabhavantyahar-agame ratryagame praliyante tatraivavyakta-sanjnake

The unmanifested turns into manifestations at the dawn of [Brahma's] day; And merges back into the unmanifested at the dusk of [Brahma's] Night.

bhuta-gramah sa evayam bhutva bhutva praliyate ratryagame 'vashah partha prabhavatyahar-agame

Multitude of beings repeatedly manifest [at the dawn of Brahma's Day] only to be unmanifested, O Pritha's son, helplessly [at the dusk of Brahma's Night]

paras tasmat tu bhavo 'nyo 'vyakto 'vyaktat sanatanah yah sa sarveshu bhuteshu nashyatsu na vinashyati

But apart from this [cycle of destructive] manifestations, there is an eternal manifestation; Where once manifested, one is never annihilated.

avyakto 'kshara ityuktas tam ahuh paramam gatim yam prapya na nivartante tad dhama paramam mama

That Manifest-less [Realm beyond Brahma] is the Ultimate Path [of every Yogi]; Going where no one ever returns to any realm, that is My Supreme Abode.

purushah sa parah partha bhaktya labhyas tvananyaya yasyantah-sthani bhutani yena sarvam idam tatam

That Supreme Divine Personality, O Pritha's son, is the only ONE worthy of acheiving by unswerving devotion; In whom all beings abide and who prevades in every being.

yatra kale tvanavrittim avrittim chaiva yoginah prayata yanti tam kalam vakshyami bharatarshabha

The periods that signify [whether] a Yogi will return or not return [to this mortal realm]; After departing here, is as follows, O Bull of Bharats.

agnir jyotir ahah shuklah shan-masa uttarayanam tatra prayata gachchhanti brahma brahma-vido janah

Sunlite Moon's fornight [Shukla paksh] & six months of Sun's northward movement [Uttarayan]; Deparing during this period, the knowledgeable Yogis go to the Eternal.

dhumo ratris tatha krishnah shan-masa dakshinayanam tatra chandramasam jyotir yogi prapya nivartate

Foggy dark fortnight [Krishna Paksh] & six months of Sun's southward movement [Dakshinayan]; Departing during this period, Moonlite Yogis return [to this mortal realm].

shukla-krishne gati hyete jagatah shashvate mate ekaya yatyanavrittim anyayavartate punah

These two paths, Shukla & Krishna [Lit & Dark], are the eternal exits of realms; One leads to liberation [Moksh], while the other leads to rebirth.

naite sriti partha janan yogi muhyati kashchana tasmat sarveshu kaleshu yoga-yukto bhavarjuna

Knowing these two paths, O Pritha's Son, Yogisa rreis never deluded; So at all times remain devoted to Yoga, O Arjun.

vedeshu yajneshu tapahsu chaiva daneshu yat punya-phalam pradishtam atyeti tat sarvam idam viditva yogi param sthanam upaiti chadyam

Vedic recitations, Yajna [Fire Rituals], Austerities, Charities; Appreciating all the benefits therein, a Yogi finally surpasses to achieve the Supreme Primeval Abode.

Chapter 09

shri bhagavan uvacha idam tu te guhyatamam pravakshyamyanasuyave jnanam vijnana-sahitam yaj jnatva mokshyase 'shubhat

The Lord Says: Now I shall reveal, inarguably the most profound knowledge with explanation, knowing which will save you from inauspiciousness.

raja-vidya raja-guhyam pavitram idam uttamam pratyakshavagamam dharmyam su-sukham kartum avyayam

Noble knowledge that is Royaly profound & purest; Practical, virtuous, easily adaptable and infallible.

ashraddadhanah purusha dharmasyasya parantapa aprapya mam nivartante mrityu-samsara-vartmani

Nonbelievers of [Sanatan] Dharma, O tormentor of foes; Will not attain Me, and be bound to this mortal realm by rebirth.

maya tatam idam sarvam jagad avyakta-murtina mat-sthani sarva-bhutani na chaham teshvavasthitah

I pervade this entire creation in My unmanifested form; All manifestations depend on Me, I do not on depend them.

na cha mat-sthani bhutani pashya me yogam aishwaram bhuta-bhrin na cha bhuta-stho mamatma bhuta-bhavanah

Remaining independent of all manifestations, through my Divine Yoga; Creating & sustaining them, yet remaining unaffected by them.

yathakasha-sthito nityam vayuh sarvatra-go mahan tatha sarvani bhutani mat-sthanityupadharaya

Just as the mighty winds everywhere, exists within the sky; Similarly, understand that all manifested exist in Me.

sarva-bhutani kaunteya prakritim yanti mamikam kalpa-kshaye punas tani kalpadau visrijamyaham

All manifested, O Kunti's Son, in this creation merges into Me at the end of every Kalp [of Brahma's Night] & recreated at the beginning [of Brahma's Day].

prakritim svam avashtabhya visrijami punah punah bhuta-gramam imam kritsnam avasham prakriter vashat

Creation's my dominion, which I recreate time and time again; The whole aggregate of manifestations, surrendered to their own inherent nature.

na cha mam tani karmani nibadhnanti dhananjaya udasina-vad asinam asaktam teshu karmasu

Those actions [of recreation], O Victor of Wealth, do not bind Me; I remain indifferent and unaffected by those actions.

mayadhyakshena prakritih suyate sa-characharam hetunanena kaunteya jagad viparivartate

Under My supervision, Nature creates everything that is movable & immovable; Owing to which, O Kunti's son, this universe functions.

avajananti mam mudha manushim tanum ashritam param bhavam ajananto mama bhuta-maheshvaram

To the deluded, I am unrecognizable in this human form; They are unable to see My Divinity and know that I am the Lord of all Beings.

moghasha mogha-karmano mogha-jnana vichetasah rakshasim asurim chaiva prakritim mohinim shritah

Mindlessly [involved] in harmful expectations, harmful actions, & harmful knowledge; Behave as if possessed by fiendish & demonic nature.

mahatmanas tu mam partha daivim prakritim ashritah bhajantyananya-manaso jnatva bhutadim avyayam

The great souls possessing godly nature, O Pritha's Son, worship Me with complete devotion, knowing Me to be the Creator.

satatam kirtayanto mam yatantash cha dridha-vratah namasyantash cha mam bhaktya nitya-yukta upasate

[The great souls] Always glorify Me with determination; Bow with devotion, and constantly worship Me.

jnana-yajnena chapyanye yajanto mam upasate ekatvena prithaktvena bahudha vishvato-mukham

Others meditate upon Me through knowledge & wisdom; As a whole Me or in separate forms as multi-faceted as the universe.

aham kratur aham yajnah svadhaham aham aushadham mantro 'ham aham evajyam aham agnir aham hutam pitaham asya jagato mata dhata pitamahah vedyam pavitram omkara rik sama yajur eva cha

I am Kritu [Vedic ritual], I am Yajna [Fire-Sacrifice], I am Swadha [Oblation], I am the Aushadam [Medicinal herbs], I am Mantra [Chants], I am Ajyam [Clarified Butter], I am Agni [Sacred Fire], I am Hutam [Offering].

prakritim svam avashtabhya visrijami punah punah bhuta-gramam imam kritsnam avasham prakriter vashat

I am the Universal Father, Mother, Sustainer & Grandsire; The sacred syllable Omkar [Om/Aum] worth learning and the Vedas [Rig, Sama, Yajur].

gatir bharta prabhuh sakshi nivasah sharanam suhrit prabhavah pralayah sthanam nidhanam bijam avyayam

I am the Ultimate Path, Sustainer, Lord, Witness, Abode, Refuge, and Friend; The Origin, End, Stratum, Storage & Imperishable Seed.

tapamyaham aham varsham nigrihnamyutsrijami cha amritam chaiva mrityush cha sad asach chaham arjuna

My warmth makes rain that I withhold [as clouds] before allowing it to fall; I am immortality as well as death, I am matter as well as anti-matter, O Arjun.

trai-vidya mam soma-pah puta-papa yajnair ishtva svar-gatim prarthayante te punyam asadya surendra-lokam ashnanti divyan divi deva-bhogan

Knowers of [three] Vedas, Soma drinkers, [worship] Me to cleanse their sins through Yajna [fire-sacrifice] & reach Heavens; As a result of their pious deeds, upon reaching realm of Indra they relish divine luxuries enjoyed by Demi-gods.

te tam bhuktva swarga-lokam vishalam kshine punye martya-lokam vishanti evam trayi-dharmam anuprapanna gatagatam kama-kama labhante

They [knowers of 3 Vedas] enjoy the spacious heaven, but upon exhausting their pious deeds return to this mortal realm; Such knowers of [three] Vedas, desirous of enjoyments, keep circling back & forth.

ananyash chintayanto mam ye janah paryupasate tesham nityabhiyuktanam yoga-kshemam vahamyaham

[But] Those who devoutly meditate upon Me, only worshipping Me; My such staunch devotees are blessed with My never ending Yoga [bliss].

ye 'pyanya-devata-bhakta yajante shraddhayanvitah te 'pi mam eva kaunteya yajantyavidhi-purvakam

Even those devotees who faithfully worship other Demi-gods, indirectly worship Me, O Kunti's son, however through incorrect methods.

aham hi sarva-yajnanam bhokta cha prabhureva cha na tu mam abhijananti tattvenatash chyavanti te

As I alone am the Lord & beneficiary of all Yajnas [sacrifices]; Those who do not realize this truth, they fall [back to this mortal realm].

yanti deva-vrata devan pitrin yanti pitri-vratah bhutani yanti bhutejya yanti mad-yajino 'pi mam

Those who worship Demigods reach Demigods, those who worship Ancestors reach Ancestors, those who worship Mortals reach Mortals; My worshippers reach Me.

patram pushpam phalam toyam yo me bhaktya prayachchhati tadaham bhaktyupahritam ashnami prayatatmanah

Leaf [Betel leaf], flower, fruit [or Betel-nut], or water whosoever offers Me; Such sincere offering by a devout I accept readily.

yat karoshi yad ashnasi yaj juhoshi dadasi yat yat tapasyasi kaunteya tat kurushva mad-arpanam

Whatever you do, eat, sacrifice [as oblation], donate and endure as auterities, O Kunti's son, dedicate them to Me.

shubhashubha-phalair evam mokshyase karma-bandhanaih sannyasa-yoga-yuktatma vimukto mam upaishyasi

You shall be freed from all, auspicious or inauspicious, results arising from your actions [when you dedicate them to Me]; And as a liberated renunciated Yogi, you shall reach Me.

samo 'ham sarva-bhuteshu na me dveshyo 'sti na priyah ye bhajanti tu mam bhaktya mayi te teshu chapyaham

To Me all beings are equal, I am neither inimical nor partial to anyone; But those who worship Me with devotion, they are in Me & I in them.

api chet su-duracharo bhajate mam ananya-bhak sadhur eva sa mantavyah samyag vyavasito hi sah

Even if a vilest sinner worships Me with true devotion; He should be regarded as a rightly resolved pious person.

kshipram bhavati dharmatma shashvach-chhantim nigachchhati kaunteya pratijanihi na me bhaktah pranashyati

Soon he [rightly resolved sinner] becomes a virtuous soul eligible for Divine Path; O Kunti's son, know this, My devotees never perish.

mam hi partha vyapashritya ye 'pi syuh papa-yonayah striyo vaishyas tatha shudras te 'pi yanti param gatim

If I am, O Pritha's son, sought as a refuge by sinners, women, traders and menials, they attain the Divine Path.

kim punar brahmanah punya bhakta rajarshayas tatha anityam asukham lokam imam prapya bhajasva mam

Needless to say that pious Brahmins, pious Kingly Sages; Transiting through this joyless world, are all devoted to Me.

man-mana bhava mad-bhakto mad-yaji mam namaskuru mam evaishyasi yuktvaivam atmanam mat-parayanah

Thinking about Me, devoted to Me, worshipping Me, bowing to Me; Being completely absorbed in Me, surely you will come to Me.

Chapter 10

shri bhagavan uvacha bhuya eva maha-baho shrinu me paramam vachah yatte 'ham priyamanaya vakshyami hita-kamyaya

The Lord says: Listen closely, O Mighty-armed, to my Divine teachings; Since you are delighted with it, so desiring your welfare I shall speak.

na me viduh sura-ganah prabhavam na maharshayah aham adir hi devanam maharshinam cha sarvashah

Neither the Demigods know my origin nor the Sages, I am the origin of Demigods, Sages & everything.

yo mamajam anadim cha vetti loka-maheshvaram asammudhah sa martyeshu sarva-papaih pramuchyate

Who knows Me to be unborn, beginningless and Supreme Lord of the Universe, He is undeluded amongst mortals will be freed from all sins.

buddhir jnanam asammohah kshama satyam damah shamah sukham duhkham bhavo 'bhavo bhayam chabhayameva cha

Reason, knowledge, non-delusion, forgiveness, truthfulness, restraint, serenity, joy, sorrow, life, death, fear & courage,

ahinsa samata tushtis tapo danam yasho 'yashah bhavanti bhava bhutanam matta eva prithag-vidhah

non-violence, equanimity, benevolence, fame and infamy - All these various qualities in humans arise from Me alone.

maharshayah sapta purve chatvaro manavas tatha mad-bhava manasa jata yesham loka imah prajah

The seven Maharishis [Great Sages] and the four Manus, they were all wished into being by Me and are the progenitors of the people of this world.

etam vibhutim yogam cha mama yo vetti tattvatah so 'vikampena yogena yujyate natra sanshayah

He who comprehends the divinity & the prowess of My glorious Yoga; Is undoubtedly, steadily united with Me.

aham sarvasya prabhavo mattah sarvam pravartate iti matva bhajante mam budha bhava-samanvitah

I am the originator of all creation and all its functions; Hence the wise worship Me with loving devotion.

mach-chitta mad-gata-prana bodhayantah parasparam kathayantash cha mam nityam tushyanti cha ramanti cha

Remembering Me, dedicating their life [to create awareness] about Me; They derive satisfaction in spreading My teachings to others.

tesham satata-yuktanam bhajatam priti-purvakam dadami buddhi-yogam tam yena mam upayanti te

To them [preachers], constantly immersed in My devotion out of love; I give them the divine knowledge to attain Me.

tesham evanukampartham aham ajnana-jam tamah nashayamyatma-bhava-stho jnana-dipena bhasvata

I benevolently destroy the darkness of ignorance dwelling in them [preachers] by alighting the lamp of knowledge.

arjuna uvacha param brahma param dhama pavitram paramam bhavan purusham shashvatam divyam adi-devam ajam vibhum

Arjun Says: You are Supreme Brahman, Supreme Destination, Supremely Pure, Eternal Divine Being, Primal, Unborn, and all-pervading God.

ahus tvam rishayah sarve devarshir naradas tatha asito devalo vyasah svayam chaiva bravishi me

The one mentioned by the great sages like Narad, Asit, Deval, and Vyas - by your own admission to me.

sarvam etad ritam manye yan mam vadasi keshava na hi te bhagavan vyaktim vidur deva na danavah

I believe everything you told me, O Slayer of Keshi, Neither the Demigods nor the Demons, know your Divine form.

swayam evatmanatmanam vettha tvam purushottama bhuta-bhavana bhutesha deva-deva jagat-pate

Only you yourself know about yourself, O Supreme Being; Creator & Lord of all beings, God of the Demigods, Ruler of the Universe.

vaktum arhasyasheshena divya hyatma-vibhutayah yabhir vibhutibhir lokan imams tvam vyapya tishthasi

You alone can describe Your Divine Opulences with which You pervade and reside in this whole Universe.

katham vidyam aham yogins tvam sada parichintayan keshu keshu cha bhaveshu chintyo 'si bhagavan maya

O Master of Yoga, how shall I forever visualize You? Which aspect of Your various facets should I mediate upon?

vistarenatmano yogam vibhutim cha janardana bhuyah kathaya triptir hi shrinvato nasti me 'mritam

As you describe the Glories of Your Yoga, O Janardan, I again remain unsatiated and want to hear more of this nectar.

shri bhagavan uvacha hanta te kathayishyami divya hyatma-vibhutayah pradhanyatah kuru-shreshtha nastyanto vistarasya me

The Lord Replies: Sure, now I shall describe My divine attributes; But only the most prominent ones, O Best of Kurus, because they are unlimited.

aham atma gudakesha sarva-bhutashaya-sthitah aham adish cha madhyam cha bhutanam anta eva cha

I am the life force with which the heart beats, O Gudakesh, I am the beginning, the middle and also the end of all beings.

adityanam aham vishnur jyotisham ravir anshuman marichir marutam asmi nakshatranam aham shashi

Amongst the Sons of Aditi I am Vishnu; Amongst the luminous I am the Sun, Amongst the wind I am Marichi, Amongst Constellations I am the Moon

vedanam sama-vedo 'smi devanam asmi vasavah indriyanam manash chasmi bhutanam asmi chetana

Sama Veda amongst Vedas, Indra amongst Demigods; Amongst senses the Mind, amongst living beings Cognizance

rudranam shankarash chasmi vittesho yaksha-rakshasam vasunam pavakash chasmi meruh shikharinam aham

Amongst Rudras I am Shankar, amongst demons Kuber; Amongst Vasus I am Agni [Fire-god], amongst mountains I am Meru.

purodhasam cha mukhyam mam viddhi partha brihaspatim senaninam aham skandah sarasam asmi sagarah

Amongst priests & chiefs, O Pritha's Son, I am the Brihaspati; Amongst Generals I am Skanda, amongst reservoirs the Ocean.

maharshinam bhrigur aham giram asmyekam aksharam yajnanam japa-yajno 'smi sthavaranam himalayah

Amongst the great sages I am Rishi Bhrigu, Amongst mono-syllables Aum [OM]; Amongst rituals Jap [repetition of mantras], amongst immovable Himalayas.

ashvatthah sarva-vrikshanam devarshinam cha naradah gandharvanam chitrarathah siddhanam kapilo munih

Amongst the trees I am Ashvattha [pipal], amongst the Divine Sages I am Narada; Amongst Gandharvas I am Chitraratha and amongst Siddhas I am Sage Kapil.

uchchaihshravasam ashvanam viddhi mam amritodbhavam airavatam gajendranam naranam cha naradhipam

Amongst horses know Me as Uchchaishrava born from ocean churning [Sagar Manthan]; Amongst lordly elephants know Me as Airavat and amongst men I am the King.

ayudhanam aham vajram dhenunam asmi kamadhuk prajanash chasmi kandarpah sarpanam asmi vasukih

Amongst weapons know Me as Vajra [thunderbolt], Kamdhenu amongst cows; Kandarp [Kaamdev] amongst progenitors & Vasuki amongst serpents.

anantash chasmi naganam varuno yadasam aham pitrinam aryama chasmi yamah sanyamatam aham

Amongst snakes know Me as Anant, Varuna amongst water beings; Aryama amongst Pritris [departed ancestors] & Yama amongst moral codes. [Lord of Death] amongst enforcers

prahladash chasmi daityanam kalah kalayatam aham mriganam cha mrigendro 'ham vainateyash cha pakshinam

Amongst Daityas know Me as Prahlad, Time amongst reckoners; Lion amongst animals, Vainateya [Garud or Eagle] amongst birds.

pavanah pavatam asmi ramah shastra-bhritam aham jhashanam makarash chasmi srotasam asmi jahnavi

Amongst moving know Me as wind, Rama amongst warriors; Dolphin amongst fish & Ganges amongst springs.

sarganam adir antash cha madhyam chaivaham arjuna adhyatma-vidya vidyanam vadah pravadatam aham

Of the Worlds I am the origin, middle and end; O Arjun, Amongst sciences, the science of Spirituality and amongst debators, the logical conclusion.

aksharanam a-karo 'smi dvandvah samasikasya cha aham evakshayah kalo dhataham vishvato-mukhah

Amongst letters I am A, and the [grammatical] link between compounds; I am the everlasting Time, the multifaceted Sustainer.

mrityuh sarva-harash chaham udbhavash cha bhavishyatam kirtih shrir vak cha narinam smritir medha dhritih kshama

I am Death of all existance & Seed of all future I am; Amongst feminine qualities I am fame, prosperity, eloquence, memory, wisdom, constancy, and forebearance.

brihat-sama tatha samnam gayatri chhandasam aham masanam marga-shirsho 'ham ritunam kusumakarah

I am Brihat-Sama amongst hymns of Sama Veda, Gayatri [mantra] amongst poetic meters; Margashish amongst months, Spring amongst seasons.

dyutam chhalayatam asmi tejas tejasvinam aham jayo 'smi vyavasayo 'smi sattvam sattvavatam aham

I am the trickster amongst gamblers, splendor of splendid; Success of strugglers, virtue of virtuous.

vrishninam vasudevo 'smi pandavanam dhananjayah muninam apyaham vyasah kavinam ushana kavih

Amongst the Vrishnis I am Vasudeva; Dhananjay [Arjun] amongst Pandavas; Vyas amongst silent sages, Shukracharya amongst poets.

dando damayatam asmi nitir asmi jigishatam maunam chaivasmi guhyanam jnanam jnanavatam aham

Amongst staves I am sceptre, strategy amongst ambitious; Silence amongst secrets, knowledge amongst wise.

yach chapi sarva-bhutanam bijam tad aham arjuna na tad asti vina yat syan maya bhutam characharam

That seed of all living beings I am, O Arjun, None moving or unmoving being exists without Me.

nanto 'sti mama divyanam vibhutinam parantapa esha tuddeshatah prokto vibhuter vistaro maya

Unlimited are My Divine Attributes, O tormentor of foes; The ones I mentioned is just a minuscule account of My Divinity.

yad yad vibhutimat sattvam shrimad urjitam eva va tat tad evavagachchha tvam mama tejo 'nsha-sambhavam

Whichever being that is glorious, prosperous, and powerful; know it to spring from but a spark of my splendor.

atha va bahunaitena kim jnatena tavarjuna vishtabhyaham idam kritsnam ekanshena sthito jagat

Apart from these, what good would it be knowing about My other Divine Attributes, O Arjun? Suffice to know that I prevade & sustain this whole Universe with just a fraction of My being.

Chapter 11

arjuna uvacha mad-anugrahaya paramam guhyam adhyatma-sanjnitam yat tvayoktam vachas tena moho 'yam vigato mama

Arjun says: The profound spiritual knowledge, that you have revealed out of compassion, has dispelled my delusion.

bhavapyayau hi bhutanam shrutau vistarasho maya tvattah kamala-patraksha mahatmyam api chavyayam

I have heard manifesting unmanifesting of beings in great detail O Lotus Eyed, Your Eternal Majesty.

evam etad yathattha tvam atmanam parameshvara drashtum ichchhami te rupam aishwaram purushottama

As You have described Yourself, I desire to see that Divine form of Yours, O Supreme Being.

manyase yadi tach chhakyam maya drashtum iti prabho yogeshvara tato me tvam darshayatmanam avyayam

If you consider it is possible for me to see it, O Lord of Yogas, then please show me Your Universal from.

shri-bhagavan uvacha pashya me partha rupani shatasho 'tha sahasrashah nana-vidhani divyani nana-varnakritini cha

The Lord replies: Behold, O Pritha's son, My forms in hundreds of thousands of Divine varities, shapes, and colors.

pashyadityan vasun rudran ashvinau marutas tatha bahuny adrishta-purvani pashyashcharyani bharata

Behold the Aditiyas, Vasus, Rudras, Ashwins, & Maruts; And many never before seen wondrous forms, O Arjun.

ihaika-stham jagat kritsnam pashyadya sa-characharam mama dehe gudakesha yach chanyad drashtum ichchhasi

Behold the Universe of the moving & the unmoving assembled together in My Universal form, O Gudakesh, and all else you desire to see.

na tu mam shakyase drashtum anenaiva sva-chakshusha divyam dadami te chakshuh pashya me yogam aishwaram

But you would be unable to view My Cosmic form with your normal vision; So I bestow on you divine vision, behold My Opulent Yoga.

sanjaya uvacha evam uktva tato rajan maha-yogeshvaro harih darshayam asa parthaya paramam rupam aishwaram

Sanjay says: O King, the Supreme Lord of Yoga, Hari showed to Prath His Supreme Divine forms.

aneka-vaktra-nayanam   anekadbhuta-darshanam aneka-divyabharanam divyanekodyatayudham

There were innumerable faces & eyes and many wondrous scences, divine ornaments and weapons.

divya-malyambara-dharam   divya-gandhanulepanam sarvashcharya-mayam devam anantam vishvato-mukham

Wearing divine garlands and garments, annointed with divine scents; All wonderful, resplendant, infinite multi-faced.

divi surya-sahasrasya bhaved yugapad utthita yadi bhah sadrishi sa syad bhasas tasya mahatmanah

If the sky was lit with a thousand suns together, It would scarcely match the brilliance of that Mighty Being.

tatraika-stham jagat kritsnam pravibhaktam anekadha apashyad deva-devasya sharire pandavas tada

There gathered together in that Universal form, Pandava [Arjun] saw unlimited cosmic expansions in the body of the God of Demigods.

tatah sa vismayavishto hrishta-roma dhananjayah pranamya shirasa devam kritanjalir abhashata

Then awe-struck with hair standing on end, Dhananjaya, Bowing his head to the resplendent One with folded hands spoke.

arjuna uvacha pashyami devans tava deva dehe sarvans tatha bhuta-vishesha-sanghan brahmanam isham kamalasana-stham rishinsh cha sarvan uragansh cha divyan

Arjun says: I see the Devas [Demigods], O God, in Thy body and assemblage of all other beings, Lord Brahma the on lotus seat and all the sages and celestial serpents.

aneka-bahudara-vaktra-netram pashyami tvam sarvato 'nanta-rupam nantam na madhyam na punas tavadim pashyami vishveshvara vishva-rupa

I see Your boundless form all around with innumerable arms, bellies, mouths and eyes, in Your Universal form has no end nor middle nor beginning, O Lord of the Universe.

kiritinam gadinam chakrinam cha tejo-rashim sarvato diptimantam pashyami tvam durnirikshyam samantad diptanalarka-dyutim aprameyam

Adorning a crown, mace, and discus, illuminating everywhere; I only see You all around, shinning brightly like innumerable blazing suns, blindingly dazzling.

tvam aksharam paramam veditavyam tvam asya vishvasya param nidhanam tvam avyayah shashvata-dharma-gopta sanatanas tvam purusho mato me

You are the Supreme, Imperishable, worthy to be known, You are The supreme Refuge of the universe. You are the undying Guardian of the eternal Dharma, The Ancient Being, such is my conviction

anadi-madhyantam ananta-viryam ananta-bahum shashi-surya-netram pashyami tvam dipta-hutasha-vaktram sva-tejasa vishvam idam tapantam

Without a beginning, middle or end, of infinite power, Of countless hands and eyes shinning like the sun and moon, I see You with a mouth breathing fire, that warms this Universe.

dyav a-prithivyor idam antaram hi vyaptam tvayaikena dishash cha sarvah drishtvadbhutam rupam ugram tavedam loka-trayam pravyathitam mahatman

The space between heaven and earth certainly is pervaded by You alone in all the directions; Seeing Your wondrous scary form The worlds are trembling, O Mighty Being.

ami hi tvam sura-sangha vishanti kechid bhitah pranjalayo grinanti svastity uktva maharshi-siddha-sanghah stuvanti tvam stutibhih pushkalabhih

All the Demigods are surrendering & merging into You. Some of them scared are hailing You with folded hands. Hosts of great Sages & Siddhas are praying to You with Vedic hymns seeking peace.

rudraditya vasavo ye cha sadhya vishve 'shvinau marutash choshmapash cha gandharva-yakshasura-siddha-sangha vikshante tvam vismitash chaiva sarve

All the various manifestations of Lord Shiva, the Adityas, the Vasus, the Sadhyas, the Visvedevas, the two Ashwins, the Maruts, the Ancestors, the Gandharvas, the Yakshas, the Asuras and the Siddhas are beholding You in wonder.

rupam mahat te bahu-vaktra-netram maha-baho bahu-bahuru-padam bahudaram bahu-danshtra-karalam drishtva lokah pravyathitas tathaham

Seeing Your immense form with its innumerable mouths, eyes, arms, feet, bellies, and terrifying teeth, O Mighty-armed, has frightened me as well as all the worlds.

nabhah-sprisham diptam aneka-varnam vyattananam dipta-vishala-netram drishtva hi tvam pravyathitantar-atma dhritim na vindami shamam cha vishno

Your sky touching form with its various colors, gaping mouths, and blazing eyes has set my heart trembling, I am losing my calm and steadiness, O Vishnu.

danshtra-karalani cha te mukhani drishtvaiva kalanala-sannibhani disho na jane na labhe cha sharma prasida devesha jagan-nivasa

Seeing Your terrifying mouths with their fiery deadly teeth, I have lost all equilibirium nor find refuge; Please calm down, O Lord of Lords, Abode of the Universe.

ami cha tvam dhritarashtrasya putrah sarve sahaivavani-pala-sanghaih bhishmo dronah suta-putras tathasau sahasmadiyair api yodha-mukhyaih

I see all the sons of Dhritarashtra, along with their allied kings, including Bheeshma, Dronacharya, Karn, and also the generals from our side,

vaktrani te tvaramana vishanti danshtra-karalani bhayanakani kechid vilagna dashanantareshu sandrishyante churnitair uttamangaih

rushing headlong into your fearsome mouths. I see some with their heads smashed between your terrible teeth.

yatha nadinam bahavo 'mbu-vegah samudram evabhimukha dravanti tatha tavami nara-loka-vira vishanti vaktrany abhivijvalanti

Like the torrents of rivers flow into the ocean, so do all the great warriors rush into Your many blazing mouths.

yatha pradiptam jvalanam patanga vishanti nashaya samriddha-vegah tathaiva nashaya vishanti lokas tavapi vaktrani samriddha-vegah

Just as moths rush towards their destruction by going headlong into a blazing fire; So too are the worlds rushing into Your mouths.

lelihyase grasamanah samantal lokan samagran vadanair jvaladbhih tejobhir apurya jagat samagram bhasas tavograh pratapanti vishno

Slurping as You devour worlds with your blazing mouths; Scorching the whole Universe with their fierce rays, O Vishnu

akhyahi me ko bhavan ugra-rupo namo 'stu te deva-vara prasida vijnatum ichchhami bhavantam adyam na hi prajanami tava pravrittim

Tell me, who You are as this fierce form? Accept my obeisance O Lord of Lords, bless me. I desire to know the reason of Your Primal form and its purpose.

shri-bhagavan uvacha kalo 'smi loka-kshaya-krit pravriddho lokan samahartum iha pravrittah rite 'pi tvam na bhavishyanti sarve ye 'vasthitah pratyanikeshu yodhah

The Lord replies: I am Time, World's Mighty Destroyer; I am here for destruction. Even without your participation, these warriors in opposing armies will be slain.

tasmat tvam uttishtha yasho labhasva jitva shatrun bhunkshva rajyam samriddham mayaivaite nihatah purvam eva nimitta-matram bhava savya-sachin

Therefore arise to gain fame by defeating your enemies and enjoy prosperous kingdom; I have already slain them, you merely be the pretext [of their deaths], O Savyasachin.

dronam cha bhishmam cha jayadratham cha karnam tathanyan api yodha-viran maya hatams tvam jahi ma vyathishtha yudhyasva jetasi rane sapatnan

Drona, Bhishma, Jayadrath, Karna and other valiant warriors have already been slain by Me, do not tremble; Fight, you will vanquish the enemy in battle.

sanjaya uvacha etach chhrutva vachanam keshavasya kritanjalir vepamanah kiriti namaskritva bhuya evaha krishnam sa-gadgadam bhita-bhitah pranamya

Sanjay says: Hearing Keshav's words, the crested [Arjun] tremblingly with joined palms bowed before Lord Krishna and overwhelmed with fear spoke chokingly.

arjuna uvacha sthane hrishikesha tava prakirtya jagat prahrishyaty anurajyate cha rakshansi bhitani disho dravanti sarve namasyanti cha siddha-sanghah

Arjun says: Aptly, O Hrishikesh [Master of Senses], in Your praise this world revels and rejoices; The Rakshasas frightened flee in all direction and the Siddhas salute You.

kasmach cha te na nameran mahatman gariyase brahmano 'py
adi-kartre ananta devesha jagan-nivasa tvam aksharam sad-asat tat
param yat

And why shouldn't they [Siddhas] bow to You, O Mighty Being,
You are orginator of Brahma, O Infinite Lord of Lords and Abode
of the Universe, You are the Imperishable, Beyond Manifested &
Non-manifested.

tvam adi-devah purushah puranas tvam asya vishvasya param
nidhanam vettasi vedyam cha param cha dhama tvaya tatam vishvam
ananta-rupa

You are Primal God and Ancient Being, You are the supreme
Abode of this world. The Knower worth knowing and Abode Supreme,
this world is pervaded by Your infinite forms.

vayur yamo 'gnir varunah shashankah prajapatis tvam
prapitamahash cha namo namas te 'stu sahasra-kritvah punash cha
bhuyo 'pi namo namas te

You are Vayu [the god of wind], Yamraj [the god of death], Agni
[the god of fire], Varun [the god of water], and Chandra [the
Moon-god]. You are the creator Brahma, and the Grandsire of all
beings. I offer my salutations unto you a thousand times, again and
again.

namah purastad atha prishthatas te namo 'stu te sarvata eva sarva
ananta-viryamita-vikramas tvam sarvam samapnoshi tato 'si sarvah

Obeisances to You from front and rear, obeisances to You from all
around; You are the infinitely mighty energy powering everyone and
everything.

sakheti matva prasabham yad uktam he krishna he yadava he
sakheti ajanata mahimanam tavedam maya pramadat pranayena vapi

Considering You as a friend, I have informally addressed You as O
Krishna, O Yadav, O Friend either negligently or affectionately.

yach chavahasartham asat-krito 'si vihara-shayyasana-bhojaneshu eko 'tha vapy achyuta tat-samaksham tat kshamaye tvam aham aprameyam

And frivolously, if I have ever offended You in any way, while playing, resting, sitting, eating, either alone or in company, O infallible one, for all that I seek Your forgiveness.

pitasi lokasya characharasya tvam asya pujyash cha gurur gariyan na tvat-samo 'sty abhyadhikah kuto 'nyo loka-traye 'py apratima-prabhava

You are the Father of this Universe, of all moving & unmoving beings, Venerable Greatest Guru; Your equal does not exist in the three worlds, how can there be someone superior, O Invincible.

tasmat pranamya pranidhaya kayam prasadaye tvam aham isham idyam piteva putrasya sakheva sakhyuh priyah priyayarhasi deva sodhum

Therefore, O adorable Lord, bowing deeply and prostrating before you, I implore you for your grace. As a father tolerates his son, a friend forgives his friend, and a lover pardons the beloved, please forgive me for my offences.

adrishta-purvam hrishito 'smi drishtva bhayena cha pravyathitam mano me tad eva me darshaya deva rupam prasida devesha jagan-nivasa

I rejoice at seeing this Universal form never before seen. But my mind is uneasy with fear, O God, bless me again with that same form. O Lord of Lords and Abode of the Universe.

kiritinam gadinam chakra-hastam ichchhami tvam drashtum aham tathaiva tenaiva rupena chatur-bhujena sahasra-baho bhava vishva-murte

The form wearing a crown, holding a mace & discus as before, I want to see that same You; Bless me with the same four armed form, O of thousand armed Universal Idol.

shri-bhagavan uvacha maya prasannena tavarjunedam rupam param darshitam atma-yogat tejo-mayam vishvam anantam adyam yan me tvad anyena na drishta-purvam

The Lord says: Being please with you, O Arjun, I showed you My transcendant form with the power of My Yoga; Resplendant, cosmic, infinite and primal, never before seen by anyone else except yourself.

na veda-yajnadhyayanair na danair na cha kriyabhir na tapobhir ugraih evam-rupah shakya aham nri-loke drashtum tvad anyena kuru-pravira

Neither by Vedic knowledge, nor Yajna, nor charity, nor pious acts, seeing Me in this form is possible in this human realm, except for you, O great Kuru hero.

ma te vyatha ma cha vimudha-bhavo drishtva rupam ghoram idrin mamedam vyapeta-bhih prita-manah punas tvam tad eva me rupam idam prapashya

Be neither afraid nor bewildered by this scary form of Mine; Be Fear-free and with a cheerful heart behold My old form again.

sanjaya uvacha ity arjunam vasudevas tathoktva svakam rupam darshayam asa bhuyah ashvasayam asa cha bhitam enam bhutva punah saumya-vapur mahatma

Sanjaya says: Saying so to Arjun, Vasudeva returned to His old form [Vishnu] again and to further console the awestricken [Arjun], The Mighty Soul resumed his gentle form [Krishna].

arjuna uvacha drishtvedam manusham rupam tava saumyam janardana idanim asmi samvrittah sa-chetah prakritim gatah

Arjun says: Seeing Thy gentle human form, O Janardan, I have regained my composure and am myself again.

shri-bhagavan uvacha su-durdarsham idam rupam drishtavan asi yan mama deva apy asya rupasya nityam darshana-kankshinah

The Lord says: This form of Mine that you have seen is very difficult to see, even Demigods always long to see it.

naham vedair na tapasa na danena na chejyaya shakya evam-vidho drashtum drishtavan asi mam yatha

Neither by knowing Vedas, nor with austerity, nor with charity, nor with sacrifice can this form be seen, as you saw it.

bhaktya tv ananyaya shakya aham evam-vidho 'rjuna jnatum drashtum cha tattvena praveshtum cha parantapa

Only with undivided devotion I can, O Arjun, Be known and seen; And only with the knowledge of [My] Reality can one merge into My bliss, O tormentor of foes.

mat-karma-krin mat-paramo mad-bhaktah sanga-varjitah nirvairah sarva-bhuteshu yah sa mam eti pandava

Those who actively work for attaining My bliss, My devotee, free from attachments and ill-will against all beings attains Me, O Pandava.

Chapter 12

arjuna uvacha evam satata-yukta ye bhaktas tvam paryupasate ye chapy aksharam avyaktam tesham ke yoga-vittamah

Arjun asks: Between Your ardent devotees, which are expert Yogis, those who worship You [as an idol] or those who worship Your Invincible Unmanifested form?

shri-bhagavan uvacha mayy aveshya mano ye mam nitya-yukta upasate shraddhaya parayopetas te me yuktatama matah

The Lord replies: Those who can constantly meditate upon Me by visualizing Me [as an idol], those devotees I consider highly endowed souls.

ye tv aksharam anirdeshyam avyaktam paryupasate sarvatra-gam achintyancha kuta-stham achalandhruvam

But those who worship the formless aspect of the Absolute Truth, the Invincible, the Indefinable, the Unmanifest, the All-pervading, the Unimaginable, the Immutable, the Eternal, & the immoveable by restraining their senses and being even-minded everywhere, such persons, engaged in the welfare of all beings, also attain Me.

sanniyamyendriya-gramam sarvatra sama-buddhayah te prapnuvanti mam eva sarva-bhuta-hite ratah

ditto

klesho 'dhikataras tesham avyaktasakta-chetasam avyakta hi gatir duhkham dehavadbhir avapyate

It is tumultuous to bring the mind to adapt the Unmanifested, because Unmanifested is difficult to visualize by the [manifested] embodied [humans].

ye tu sarvani karmani mayi sannyasya mat-parah ananyenaiva yogena mam dhyayanta upasate

But those who dedicate all their activities as an act of worship to Me with undivided devotion. I deliver them from the ocean of this mortal realm without delay, O Pritha's son, those who idolize Me.

tesham aham samuddharta mrityu-samsara-sagarat bhavami na chirat partha mayy aveshita-chetasam

ditto

mayy eva mana adhatsva mayi buddhim niveshaya nivasishyasi mayy eva ata urdhvam na sanshayah

By visualizing Me the mind is fixated in Me, Once fixated in Me your mind thereafter would never doubt.

atha chittam samadhatum na shaknoshi mayi sthiram abhyasa-yogena tato mam ichchhaptum dhananjaya

If you are unable to visualize Me steadily; Then keep practicing Yoga and soon you will form the habit, O Winner of Wealth.

abhyase 'py asamartho 'si mat-karma-paramo bhava mad-artham api karmani kurvan siddhim avapsyasi

If you are unable to neither meditate nor practice [Yoga], then perform actions for My sake and you shall gain perfection.

athaitad apy ashakto 'si kartum mad-yogam ashritah sarva-karma-phala-tyagam tatah kuru yatatmavan

And if even that [acting for My sake] is not possible, seeking refuge in My Yoga, perform all your tasks selfessly.

shreyo hi jnanam abhyasaj jnanad dhyanam vishishyate dhyanat karma-phala-tyagas tyagach chhantir anantaram

Knowledge is better than practice, meditation is better than knowledge, better than meditation is being selfless, as it speedily leads to peace.

adveshta sarva-bhutanam maitrah karuna eva cha nirmamo nirahankarah sama-duhkha-sukhah kshami

[Those who are] hateless, friendly & kind towards all beings, without proprietorship, egoless, equipoised in happiness or sadness, forgiving,

santushtah satatam yogi yatatma dridha-nishchayah mayy arpita-mano-buddhir yo mad-bhaktah sa me priyah

content, such determined Yogis, dedicated to Me in mind & reason, such devotees are dear to Me.

yasman nodvijate loko lokan nodvijate cha yah harshamarsha-bhayodvegair mukto yah sa cha me priyah

With whom the world is at ease and who is at ease with the world, free from pleasures, displeasures, jealousy, fear and worry, such a one is dear to Me.

anapekshah shuchir daksha udasino gata-vyathah sarvarambha-parityagi yo mad-bhaktah sa me priyah

Unexpectant, uncunningly clever, not indifferent to other's miseries; Selflessly motivated, such a devotee is dear to Me.

yo na hrishyati na dveshti na shochati na kankshati shubhashubha-parityagi bhaktiman yah sa me priyah

Who is neither edgy, nor loathing, nor lamenting, nor craving; Who is not superstitious blind follower, he is dear to Me.

samah shatrau cha mitre cha tatha manapamanayoh shitoshna-sukha-duhkheshu samah sanga-vivarjitah

Impartial to friend and enemy, fame and infamy. Impartial to winter and summer, joy and sorrow, favorable and unfavorable associates;

tulya-ninda-stutir mauni santushto yena kenachit aniketah sthira-matir bhaktiman me priyo narah

Patiently accept praise or insult while remaining reticent. Never hold grudges, such a devotee is dear to Me.

ye tu dharmyamritam idam yathoktam paryupasate shraddadhana mat-parama bhaktas te 'tiva me priyah

Whosoever faithfully follows this immortal guiding principles of Dharma, as taught, are exceedingly dear to Me.

Chapter 13

arjuna uvacha prakritim purusham chaiva kshetram kshetra-jnam eva cha etad veditum ichchhami jnanam jneyam cha keshava

Arjun asks: O Keshava, I wish to understand what is Prakriti & Purusha, what is Kshetra, who is Kshetrajna? I also wish to know what is true knowledge and its goal?

shri-bhagavan uvacha idam shariram kaunteya kshetram ity abhidhiyate etad yo vetti tam prahuh kshetra-jna iti tad-vidah

The Lord replies: This body, O Kunti's son, is the Kshetra [field of activies] and the one [soul] within who knows it is called the Kshetrayajna [knower of the field]

kshetra-jnam chapi mam viddhi sarva-kshetreshu bharata kshetra-kshetrajnayor jnanam yat taj jnanam matam mama

I am the knower of all fields [of every being], O Scion of Bharat, understanding the knower [Me] & the field [self] is true knowledge in My view.

tat kshetram yach cha yadrik cha yad-vikari yatash cha yat sa cha yo yat-prabhavash cha tat samasena me shrinu

The field [this body], its nature, its transformations, and its causes; What is the role of field-knower and his powers, I will now describe them.

rishibhir bahudha gitam chhandobhir vividhaih prithak brahma-sutra-padaish chaiva hetumadbhir vinishchitaih

Great sages have sung the truth about the field and the knower of the field in manifold ways. It has been stated in various Vedic hymns, and especially revealed in the Brahma Sutra, with sound logic and conclusive evidence.

maha-bhutany ahankaro buddhir avyaktam eva cha indriyani dashaikam cha pancha chendriya-gocharah

The great elements, reason, egoism, and the unmanifest, Senses ten plus one and five pastures of the senses.

ichchha dveshah sukham duhkham sanghatash chetana dhritih etat kshetram samasena sa-vikaram udahritam

Affection , aversion, joy and sorrow, awareness,and fortitude, this together has been briefly described as the field in its transformations.

amanitvam adambhitvam ahinsa kshantir arjavam acharyopasanam shaucham sthairyam atma-vinigrahah

Humility, simplicity, non-violence, forbearance, uprightness, Devotion to teacher, purity, stability and self-control

indriyartheshu vairagyam anahankara eva cha janma-mrityu-jara-vyadhi-duhkha-doshanudarshanam

Indifference to objects of senses, and absence of egoism, Keeping before the mind, the demerits of birth, death, decay, sickness and sorrow.

asaktir anabhishvangah putra-dara-grihadishu nityam cha sama-chittatvam ishtanishtopapattishu

Non-attachment and absence of [blind] affection for son, wife and home. Constant even-mindedness in occurrence of the desired or the undesired.

mayi chananya-yogena bhaktir avyabhicharini vivikta-desha-sevitvam aratir jana-sansadi

Unerring devotion to Me by unswerving Yoga, Living in a quiet quarter, and distaste in mixing with people.

adhyatma-jnana-nityatvam tattva-jnanartha-darshanam etaj jnanam iti proktam ajnanam yad ato 'nyatha

Constancy in learning the truthabout self and reflecting on that truth; This is called knowledge, what is opposed to it is ignorance.

jneyam yat tat pravakshyami yaj jnatvamritam ashnute anadi mat-param brahma na sat tan nasad uchyate

I shall now explain the knowable, knowing which you will enjoy immortality. The Beginningless is the Supreme Brahman, He is says to be neither being nor not-being.

sarvatah pani-padam tat sarvato 'kshi-shiro-mukham sarvatah shrutimal loke sarvam avritya tishthati

[The Supreme Brahman] has hands, feet, eyes, heads and mouths everywhere; Listening to everything that is happening everywhere in this Universe.

sarvendriya-gunabhasam sarvendriya-vivarjitam asaktam sarva-bhrich chaiva nirgunam guna-bhoktri cha

Perceiving every sensory detail, even though being devoid of any senses; Independent of any necessities or attributes, yet enjoys everything.

bahir antash cha bhutanam acharam charam eva cha sukshmatvat tad avijneyam dura-stham chantike cha tat

Within and without all moving and also unmoving beings, subtlety incomprehensible. He is faraway, yet nearby.

avibhaktam cha bhuteshu vibhaktam iva cha sthitam bhuta-bhartri cha taj jneyam grasishnu prabhavishnu cha

Indivisible yet present separately in all beings, He is also their Sustainer, Devourer and Creator.

jyotisham api taj jyotis tamasah param uchyate jnanam jneyam jnana-gamyam hridi sarvasya vishthitam

He is the source of light in all luminaries, and is entirely beyond the darkness of ignorance. He is knowledge, the object of knowledge, and the goal of knowledge. He dwells within the hearts of all living beings.

iti kshetram tatha jnanam jneyam choktam samasatah mad-bhakta etad vijnaya mad-bhavayopapadyate

I have thus revealed to you the nature of the field, the meaning of knowledge, and the object of knowledge. Only My devotees can understand this in reality, and by doing so, they attain My divine nature.

prakritim purusham chaiva viddhy anadi ubhav api vikaransh cha gunansh chaiva viddhi prakriti-sambhavan

Know that prakṛiti [material nature] and puruṣh [the individual souls] are both beginningless. Also know that all transformations of the body and the three traits of nature are produced by transacting with the material nature.

karya-karana-kartritve hetuh prakritir uchyate purushah sukha-duhkhanam bhoktritve hetur uchyate

Nature is responsible for the agency of cause & effect and the self is responsible for enjoying its pleasures & pains.

purushah prakriti-stho hi bhunkte prakriti-jan gunan karanam guna-sango 'sya sad-asad-yoni-janmasu

When the purush [individual soul] seated in prakriti [the material nature] desires to enjoy the three gunas [traits], attachment to them becomes the cause of its birth in superior and inferior wombs.

upadrashtanumanta cha bharta bhokta maheshvarah paramatmeti chapy ukto dehe 'smin purushah parah

Spectator, Permitter, Supporter, Enjoyer, and Lord residing within is the ultimate controller known as the Supreme Soul.

ya evam vetti purusham prakritim cha gunaih saha sarvatha vartamano 'pi na sa bhuyo 'bhijayate

Whosoever understands the Soul, the Nature and its three traits, regardless of their present state, they shall not be reborn.

dhyanenatmani pashyanti kechid atmanam atmana anye sankhyena yogena karma-yogena chapare

Some are able to realize the Soul within through meditation, some through knowledge and others through Karmayoga [selfless deeds].

anye tv evam ajanantah shrutvanyebhya upasate te 'pi chatitaranty eva mrityum shruti-parayanah

Those unaware of any spiritual paths, still worship [Me] by hearing from others, also cross over death by developing devotion.

yavat sanjayate kinchit sattvam sthavara-jangamam kshetra-kshetrajna-sanyogat tad viddhi bharatarshabha

Every being, whether animate or inanimate, comes into existence as a result of the union of the "field" and "Knower of the field", O Strongest of Bharats.

samam sarveshu bhuteshu tishthantam parameshvaram vinashyatsv avinashyantam yah pashyati sa pashyati

Present equally in all living beings is that Supreme Lord, The Imperishable amidst the perishable [bodies], those who realize this, see the truth.

samam pashyan hi sarvatra samavasthitam ishvaram na hinasty atmanatmanam tato yati param gatim

Knowing that the Supreme exists equally in all living beings, one does not hurt others, knowing that by hurting others, he is only hurting himself, only such souls reach salvation.

prakrityaiva cha karmani kriyamanani sarvashah yah pashyati tathatmanam akartaram sa pashyati

All actions are really preformed by the [person under the influence of three traits of] nature, and who knows that the embodied soul is just a non-actor, sees the truth.

yada bhuta-prithag-bhavam eka-stham anupashyati tata eva cha vistaram brahma sampadyate tada

When he sees diversity of beings rooted in Unity and its evolution from the same then he becomes Brahman-like.

anaditvan nirgunatvat paramatmayam avyayah sharira-stho 'pi kaunteya na karoti na lipyate

The Supreme Soul is imperishable, without beginning, and devoid of traits of nature, O Kunti's son. Although situated within the body, It neither acts, nor is It tainted by material nature.

yatha sarva-gatam saukshmyad akasham nopalipyate sarvatravasthito dehe tathatma nopalipyate

Like the subtle space, which upholds everything yet remains untainted, similarly the all pervading soul in everybody remains untainted.

yatha prakashayaty ekah kritsnam lokam imam ravih kshetram kshetri tatha kritsnam prakashayati bharata

Just as one sun illumines this whole world, so does the field-dweller [soul] illumines the whole field [body], O Bharat.

kshetra-kshetrajnayor evam antaram jnana-chakshusha bhuta-prakriti-moksham cha ye vidur yanti te param

Those who percieve the distinction between the 'Field' [Body] and the 'Knower of the body' [Soul] through the eyes of [this] knowledge and know how to liberate themselves from [the three traits] of nature, attain the Supreme.

Chapter 14

shri-bhagavan uvacha param bhuyah pravakshyami jnananam jnanam
uttamam yaj jnatva munayah sarve param siddhim ito gatah

The Lord says: I shall once again explain to you the supreme
wisdom, the best of all knowledge; by knowing which, all the great
saints attained the highest perfection.

idam jnanam upashritya mama sadharmyam agatah sarge 'pi
nopajayante pralaye na vyathanti cha

[Those who have] Surrendered & imbibed in this knowledge, are
neither materialized nor tormented at the time of recreation or
dissolution [pralay]

mama yonir mahad brahma tasmin garbham dadhamy aham
sambhavah sarva-bhutanam tato bhavati bharata

The nature [prakṛiti] is the womb.I impregnate it, wherefrom all
living beings are born.

sarva-yonishu kaunteya murtayah sambhavanti yah tasam brahma
mahad yonir aham bija-pradah pita

Every being, O Kunti's son, irrespective of their form is born from
the womb of mother Nature and I am the seeding father.

sattvam rajas tama iti gunah prakriti-sambhavah nibadhnanti
maha-baho dehe dehinam avyayam

Born along are the three traits of Nature Satva, Rajas, & Tamas, O
mighty armed, that envelop the unchangeable dweller [soul] in a body.

tatra sattvam nirmalatvat prakashakam anamayam sukha-sangena
badhnati jnana-sangena chanagha

Of these, [three traits of Nature], Satva due to its purity is
illumining and harmless. Associating with Satva unites one with joy
and knowledge, O Sinless

rajo ragatmakam viddhi trishna-sanga-samudbhavam tan
nibadhnati kaunteya karma-sangena dehinam

Associating with Rajas breeds temptations and desires, O Kunti's son, which binds the Soul, through attachment to fruitive actions.

tamas tv ajnana-jam viddhi mohanam sarva-dehinam
pramadalasya-nidrabhis tan nibadhnati bharata

Association with Tamas breeds ignorance and mesmerises everybody, and binds [the Soul] through listlessness, indolence and sleep, O Bharat.

sattvam sukhe sanjayati rajah karmani bharata jnanam avritya tu tamah pramade sanjayaty uta

Satva unites [the soul] with joy, Rajas unites [the soul] with fruitive actions, O Bharat, Tamas first blurs knowledge and then unites [the soul] with lethargy.

rajas tamash chabhibhuya sattvam bhavati bharata rajah sattvam tamash chaiva tamah sattvam rajas tatha

When Rajas and Tamas are overpowered, Satva prevails, O Bharat, when Satva and Tamas are overpowered, Rajas prevails and when Satva and Rajas as overpowered, Tamas prevails.

sarva-dvareshu dehe 'smin prakasha upajayate jnanam yada tada vidyad vivriddham sattvam ity uta

When all sense organs emanate radiance through knowledge and wisdom, know that Satva is predominant.

lobhah pravrittir arambhah karmanam ashamah spriha rajasy etani jayante vivriddhe bharatarshabha

Greed, activity, initiation of action, anxiety, and craving appear when Rajas is predominant, O Arjun.

aprakasho 'pravrittish cha pramado moha eva cha tamasy etani jayante vivriddhe kuru-nandana

Darkness, inactivity, heedlessness and delusion arises when Tamas predominates, O scion of Kuru.

yada sattve pravriddhe tu pralayam yati deha-bhrit tadottama-vidam lokan amalan pratipadyate

The Soul that departs from the body when Satva is predominant, acheives the highest realms of learned.

rajasi pralayam gatva karma-sangishu jayate tatha pralinas tamasi mudha-yonishu jayate

When the Soul departs with Rajas [predominating] it is reborn among other actionists, when [Soul departs] with Tamas, then it is reborn through unintelligent wombs.

karmanah sukritasyahuh sattvikam nirmalam phalam rajasas tu phalam duhkham ajnanam tamasah phalam

Outcome of action performed with when Satva is predominant is pure and stainless, when Rajas is predominant is grief, when Tamas is predominant leads to unintelligence.

sattvat sanjayate jnanam rajaso lobha eva cha pramada-mohau tamaso bhavato 'jnanam eva cha

From Satva arises knowledge, from Rajas greed, and from Tamas unintelligence, delusion and mindlessness.

urdhvam gachchhanti sattva-stha madhye tishthanti rajasah jaghanya-guna-vritti-stha adho gachchhanti tamasah

Satvic Souls rise to higher realms, Rajasic Souls remain in the middle [mortal realm of earth], and with lower qualities the Tamasic Souls falls low into unintelligent species.

nanyam gunebhyah kartaram yada drashtanupashyati gunebhyash cha param vetti mad-bhavam so 'dhigachchhati

Only upon realizing that its none other but these traits of Nature that compels one to act as per their predominance, does one merges with me.

gunan etan atitya trin dehi deha-samudbhavan janma-mrityu-jara-duhkhair vimukto 'mritam ashnute

Only after rising above the three traits of Nature, the Soul is freed from birth, death, decay, and sorrow to attain immortality.

arjuna uvacha kair lingais trin gunan etan atito bhavati prabho kim acharah katham chaitans trin gunan ativartate

Arjun asks: O Lord, what are the features of those who have surpassed the three traits of Nature? How do they conduct themselves? How does one rise above these three traits of Nature?

shri-bhagavan uvacha prakasham cha pravrittim cha moham eva cha pandava na dveshti sampravrittani na nivrittani kankshati

The Lord replies: Neither illumination [Satva], nor activity [Rajas] or delusion [Tamas] , O Pandava, affects such a person, he neither abhors it when its [trait's] present, nor craves for it when its [trait's] absent.

udasina-vad asino gunair yo na vichalyate guna vartanta ity evam yo 'vatishthati nengate

Indifferent and uninfluenced he remains unmoved and fully aware that its the three traits of Nature that are causing all the commotion.

sama-duhkha-sukhah sva-sthah sama-loshtashma-kanchanah tulya-priyapriyo dhiras tulya-nindatma-sanstutih

Equipoised in joy or sorrow, self aware, valuing equally a lump of clay, stone or gold, pleasure or displeasure, enduring equally fame or infamy

manapamanayos tulyas tulyo mitrari-pakshayoh sarvarambha-parityagi gunatitah sa uchyate

Enduring equally praise or insult, treating equally a friend or a foe, renouncing all enterprise, is called a 'Gunateet', the one who has risen above the three traits of Nature.

mam cha yo 'vyabhicharena bhakti-yogena sevate sa gunan samatityaitan brahma-bhuyaya kalpate

Whosoever serves Me with sincere devotion rises above the three modes of Nature and fit to attain Brahma [immortality].

brahmano hi pratishthaham amritasyavyayasya cha shashvatasya cha dharmasya sukhasyaikantikasya cha

Because for the Brahman [the immortal], Eternal and Infinite I am the abode, as I am the abode for the Eternal Dharma and of the Absolute Bliss.

Chapter 15

shri-bhagavan uvacha urdhva-mulam adhah-shakham ashvattham prahur avyayam chhandansi yasya parnani yas tam veda sa veda-vit

The Lord Says: [Life is] like the fig tree whose roots originate at the top and branch downwards, as recited by the knowers from leaves of the Vedas.

adhash chordhvam prasritas tasya shakha guna-pravriddha vishaya-pravalah adhash cha mulany anusantatani karmanubandhini manushya-loke

This [Fig tree's] branches spread upwards as well as downwards and are nourished by the traits of Nature; sensual organs are its buds, the Karmas [actions of the sensual organs] form the network of rootlets that binds [the Soul] to this human world.

na rupam asyeha tathopalabhyate nanto na chadir na cha sampratishtha ashvattham enam su-virudha-mulam asanga-shastrena dridhena chhittva

Its [life's fig tree's] real form, origin, end or existence is imperceptible, but this deep rooted Ashvattha [life's fig tree] must be cut down with the strong weapon of detachment.

tatah padam tat parimargitavyam yasmin gata na nivartanti bhuyah tam eva chadyam purusham prapadye yatah pravrittih prasrita purani

Then that ultimate destination must be sought, reaching which there is no returning to this cycle of birth & death; I seek refuge in that same Primeval Being, out of whom this life originated long ago.

nirmana-moha jita-sanga-dosha adhyatma-nitya vinivritta-kamah dvandvair vimuktah sukha-duhkha-sanjnair gachchhanty amudhah padam avyayam tat

Without pride or delusion, having won over the ills of attachments; Enlightened and free from desires and contradictions of joy and sorrow, the wise [Soul] reaches that Eternal Goal [Moksha].

na tad bhasayate suryo na shashanko na pavakah yad gatva na nivartante tad dhama paramam mama

Neither by sun, nor by moon, nor fire is My Supreme Abode illuminated. Having gone There, no one returns to this material world again

mamaivansho jiva-loke jiva-bhutah sanatanah manah-shashthanindriyani prakriti-sthani karshati

The eternal embodied Souls in this mortal world are My fragments, which are bound here due to their attraction toward the traits of Nature through their senses.

shariram yad avapnoti yach chapy utkramatishvarah grihitvaitani sanyati vayur gandhan ivashayat

When an embodied Soul assumes or relinquishes a body, it takes these [sensual attractions] with it like the wind carries the scent away from its origin

shrotram chakshuh sparshanam cha rasanam ghranam eva cha adhishthaya manash chayam vishayan upasevate

[The embodied Soul] Through ears, eyes, skin, tongue, nose and mind enjoys the objects.

utkramantam sthitam vapi bhunjanam va gunanvitam vimudha nanupashyanti pashyanti jnana-chakshushah

It [embodied Soul] migrates, resides, or gets entangled under the influence of three traits of Nature; But the ignorant cannot see that, only the wise can, through the lens of knowledge.

yatanto yoginash chainam pashyanty atmany avasthitam yatanto 'py akritatmano nainam pashyanty achetasah

Striving yogis too are able to realize that it [the Soul] is enshrined within their bodies. But, those who are confounded by ego are unable to realize it, even after striving.

yad aditya-gatam tejo jagad bhasayate 'khilam yach chandramasi yach chagnau tat tejo viddhi mamakam

Understand that the light in the sun which illuminates the whole world, the light in the moon and in the fire is My radiance.

gam avishya cha bhutani dharayamy aham ojasa pushnami chaushadhih sarvah somo bhutva rasatmakah

Enclosing the earth I support every being with My energy, I nourish and rejunvenate all with the nectar of life at night.

aham vaishvanaro bhutva praninam deham ashritah pranapana-samayuktah pachamy annam chatur-vidham

Becoming digestive fire in the stomach of all living beings and with the aid of inhaling and exhaling breath, I digest the food in four steps.

sarvasya chaham hridi sannivishto mattah smritir jnanam apohanam cha vedaish cha sarvair aham eva vedyo vedanta-krid veda-vid eva chaham

I am enshrined in everybody's heart, from Me comes knowledge, memory, forgetfulness. It is I, that is to be learnt through Vedas, as well as its creator and its scholar.

dvav imau purushau loke ksharash chakshara eva cha ksharah sarvani bhutani kuta-stho 'kshara uchyate

Duality exists in every being of this realm, a part which lasts and another which does not; All that is born is mortal and one that is impersihable is immortal.

uttamah purushas tv anyah paramatmety udahritah yo loka-trayam avishya bibharty avyaya ishvarah

Besides these [dualities], there is the imperishable Divine Supreme Personality, who prevades all three realms and sustains them.

yasmat ksharam atito 'ham aksharad api chottamah ato 'smi loke vede cha prathitah purushottamah

Because I am transcendental, beyond both the perishable and imperishable and the greatest; I am celebrated both in the world and in the Vedas as that Supreme Person.

yo mam evam asammudho janati purushottamam sa sarva-vid bhajati mam sarva-bhavena bharata

The wise who know Me as the Supreme Divine Personality, knows that I am all there is to know and hence worships Me whole-heartedly, O scion of Bharat.

iti guhyatamam shastram idam uktam mayanagha etad buddhva buddhiman syat krita-krityash cha bharata

This is the most profound knowledge of the Vedic scriptures, O Sinless one, and it is disclosed to you by Me. Whosoever understands this will become wise, and his endeavors will know perfection, O scion of Bharat.

Chapter 16

shri-bhagavan uvacha abhayam sattva-sanshuddhir jnana-yoga-vyavasthitih danam damash cha yajnash cha svadhyayas tapa arjavam

The Lord says: Fearlessness, self-purification through Satva lifestyle, gaining knowledge, charity, continence, Yajna [fire sacrifice], studying scriptures, austerity, and moral righteousness,

ahinsa satyam akrodhas tyagah shantir apaishunam daya bhuteshv aloluptvam mardavam hrir achapalam

Non-violence, truth, non-anger, renunciation, serenity, non-pettiness, compassion towards all beings, non-covetousness, gentleness, modesty, determined,

tejah kshama dhritih shaucham adroho nati-manita bhavanti sampadam daivim abhijatasya bharata

lustrous, forgiving, courageous, cleanliness, loyalty, non-hubristic are the virtues of those born with divine qualities, O scion of Bharat.

dambho darpo 'bhimanash cha krodhah parushyam eva cha ajnanam chabhijatasya partha sampadam asurim

Hypocrisy, ostentatious, vain, short-tempered, insolent, unintelligent, O son of Pritha, are found in those born with demonic qualities.

daivi sampad vimokshaya nibandhayasuri mata ma shuchah sampadam daivim abhijato 'si pandava

The divine qualities leads to liberation [Moksha], while the demonic qualities leads to bondage [of birth & death], worry not O Pandava, you are born with divine qualities.

dvau bhuta-sargau loke 'smin daiva asura eva cha daivo vistarashah prokta asuram partha me shrinu

Two types of people exist in this world, the divine and the demonic; The divine I have described already, now I shall describe the demonic type, O son of Pritha, so listen

pravrittim cha nivrittim cha jana na vidur asurah na shaucham napi chacharo na satyam teshu vidyate

The demonic cannot differentiate between proper or improper, they lack cleanliness, good conduct, and honesty.

asatyam apratishtham te jagad ahur anishvaram aparaspara-sambhutam kim anyat kama-haitukam

They believe that this world is unreal, without a purpose, without a God, everybody's born from and for lust and nothing else.

etam drishtim avashtabhya nashtatmano 'lpa-buddhayah prabhavanty ugra-karmanah kshayaya jagato 'hitah

With that belief [that this world is only from & for lust] they not only destroy themselves, but their narrow mindedness results in cruel deeds that threaten the well-being of the entire world.

kamam ashritya dushpuram dambha-mana-madanvitah mohad grihitvasad-grahan pravartante 'shuchi-vratah

Resigned to insatiable lust, full of hypocrisy, ostentatiousness, and hubris, the demoniac cling to their false tenets. Thus deluded, they are attracted to the impermanence and work with impure resolve.

chintam aparimeyam cha pralayantam upashritah kamopabhoga-parama etavad iti nishchitah

They are obsessed with ceaseless anxieties that only ends with their death. Completely convinced that lust and accumulation of wealth [for lust] is the highest purpose of life.

asha-pasha-shatair baddhah kama-krodha-parayanah ihante kama-bhogartham anyayenartha-sanchayan

Bound by hundreds of desires driven lust and anger, they seek to hoard riches for sensual enjoyment by unlawful means.

idam adya maya labdham imam prapsye manoratham idam astidam api me bhavishyati punar dhanam

[Demonic people believe] that now they have gotten this much wealth which will fulfill their particular desire, tomorrow they shall beget more wealth and fulfill other desires.

asau maya hatah shatrur hanishye chaparan api ishvaro 'ham aham bhogi siddho 'ham balavan sukhi

[Demonic people believe] that after refhingen they ,komeoncanat theanyonell others too, they feel they are God like, the enjoyer and perfect, all powerful and happy.

adhyo 'bhijanavan asmi ko 'nyo 'sti sadrisho maya yakshye dasyami modishya ity ajnana-vimohitah

[Demonic people believe] just because they are wealthy they are entitled, because they have connections with the affluent, there is none other like them, they perform sacrifices, give charity and make merry.

aneka-chitta-vibhranta moha-jala-samavritah prasaktah kama-bhogeshu patanti narake 'shuchau

[Demonic people are] confounded by manifold desires, caught in the net of delusion, entangled in sensual-enjoyments, they fall into foul hell.

atma-sambhavitah stabdha dhana-mana-madanvitah yajante nama-yajnais te dambhenavidhi-purvakam

Such self-conceited and self-righteous [demonic] people, full of pride and arrogance, perform ostentatious sacrifices for showing off, disregarding the rules of the scriptures.

ahankaram balam darpam kamam krodham cha sanshritah mam atma-para-deheshu pradvishanto 'bhyasuyakah

Blinded by ego, power, haughtiness, lust, and anger, the demonic hurt Me, who is present within their own body and in the bodies of other beings [they kill].

tan aham dvishatah kruran sansareshu naradhaman kshipamy ajasram ashubhan asurishv eva yonishu

These cruel, hateful, vilest and vicious of human beings, I hurl them back into demonic wombs in this mortal world, time and again.

asurim yonim apanna mudha janmani janmani mam aprapyaiva kaunteya tato yanty adhamam gatim

Such unintelligent [demonic people], birth after birth, are born through the demonic wombs and remain oblivious about Me, O Kunti's son, reaching the most abominable states of existence.

tri-vidham narakasyedam dvaram nashanam atmanah kamah krodhas tatha lobhas tasmad etat trayam tyajet

Three gates lead to this hell of self-destruction of the Soul - Lust, anger, and greed. Therefore, one should abandon all three.

etair vimuktah kaunteya tamo-dvarais tribhir narah acharaty atmanah shreyas tato yati param gatim

The man who has escaped these three gates of hell, O Kunti's son, performs acts conducive to self-realization and thus gradually attains the supreme destination.

yah shastra-vidhim utsrijya vartate kama-karatah na sa siddhim avapnoti na sukham na param gatim

He who disregards scriptural injunctions and acts according to his own whims attains neither perfection, nor happiness, nor the supreme destination.

tasmach chhastram pramanam te karyakarya-vyavasthitau jnatva shastra-vidhanoktam karma kartum iharhasi

Therefore, let the scriptures be your guiding principle in determining what should be done and what should not be done. Knowing what has been prescribed in the scriptures you have to act accordingly.

Chapter 17

arjuna uvacha ye shastra-vidhim utsrijya yajante shraddhayanvitah tesham nishtha tu ka krishna sattvam aho rajas tamah

Arjun asks: Those who [unknowingly] do not follow scriptures, yet worship with great reverence, O Krishna, is their intention Satvic, Rajasic or Tamasic?

shri-bhagavan uvacha tri-vidha bhavati shraddha dehinam sa svabhava-ja sattviki rajasi chaiva tamasi cheti tam shrinu

The Lord replies: Every human being is born with an inherent faith, it could be any one of these three - Satvic, Rajasic, or Tamasic. Let Me explain.

sattvanurupa sarvasya shraddha bhavati bharata shraddha-mayo 'yam purusho yo yach-chhraddhah sa eva sah

Each individual's faith is according to his inherent essence [from his previous life], O scion of Bharat, his faith shapes him and he shapes his faith.

yajante sattvika devan yaksha-rakshansi rajasah pretan bhuta-ganansh chanye yajante tamasa janah

Those born with Satvic traits worship Divine Gods, Rajasic worship Yakshas & Rakshasas, Tamasic worship the Ghosts & Spirits.

ashastra-vihitam ghoram tapyante ye tapo janah dambhahankara-sanyuktah kama-raga-balanvitah

Those who undergo severe austerities and penances contradicting the scriptures, performing them out of pride and egoism, they are impelled by lust and attachment,

karshayantah sharira-stham bhuta-gramam achetasah mam chaivantah sharira-stham tan viddhy asura-nishchayan

These senseless men torture the aggregate of the Elements in their body as well as Me dwelling within, are of demonic trait.

aharas tv api sarvasya tri-vidho bhavati priyah yajnas tapas tatha danam tesham bhedam imam shrinu

Even the love for food in everybody is of three types, as is the inclination for Yajna, austerity, and charity. Let Me explain their differences.

ayuh-sattva-balarogya-sukha-priti-vivardhanah rasyah snigdhah sthira hridya aharah sattvika-priyah

[Food] which grants longevity, mental peace, strength, immunity, cheerfulness, and satisfaction that is juicy, greasy, filling, and tasty is dear to the Satvic.

katv-amla-lavanaty-ushna- tikshna-ruksha-vidahinah ahara rajasasyeshta duhkha-shokamaya-pradah

[Food] which is bitter, sour, salty, spicy, pungent, dry or charred causes unhappiness, grief, and disease is dear to Rajasic

yata-yamam gata-rasam puti paryushitam cha yat uchchhishtam api chamedhyam bhojanam tamasa-priyam

[Food] which is cold, overcooked, foul-smelling, stale and leftover is dear to Tamasic.

aphalakankshibhir yajno vidhi-drishto ya ijyate yashtavyam eveti manah samadhaya sa sattvikah

[Sacrifice] Yajna performed without wishing for a boon, as prescribed and as one's duty is Satvic.

abhisandhaya tu phalam dambhartham api chaiva yat ijyate bharata-shreshtha tam yajnam viddhi rajasam

But when a Yajna is performed for a benefit or for ostentation, O scion of Bharat, it becomes Rajasic.

vidhi-hinam asrishtannam mantra-hinam adakshinam shraddha-virahitam yajnam tamasam parichakshate

Yajna performed unconventionally, without distributing food, or without chanting mantras, without donation or devotion is considered Tamasic.

deva-dwija-guru-prajna- pujanam shaucham arjavam brahmacharyam ahinsa cha shariram tapa uchyate

When worship of the Supreme Lord, the Brahmins, the spiritual master, and the learned is done with the observance of cleanliness, modesty, continence, and harmlessness then that is the austerity of the body.

anudvega-karam vakyam satyam priya-hitam cha yat svadhyayabhyasanam chaiva van-mayam tapa uchyate

Words that are unoffending, true, pleasing and positive along with regular study of Scriptures is austerity of speech

manah-prasadah saumyatvam maunam atma-vinigrahah bhava-sanshuddhir ity etat tapo manasam uchyate

Mental serenity, benevolence, silence, self-control and purity in thought is the austerity of the mind.

shraddhaya paraya taptam tapas tat tri-vidham naraih aphalakankshibhir yuktaih sattvikam parichakshate

These trio of austerities practised with ardent faith without desiring a reward by the devout is Satvic.

satkara-mana-pujartham tapo dambhena chaiva yat kriyate tad iha proktam rajasam chalam adhruvam

Austerity that is performed ostentatiously for gaining respect and recognition is Rajasic. Its benefits are unsteady and transitory.

mudha-grahenatmano yat pidaya kriyate tapah parasyotsadanartham va tat tamasam udahritam

Austerity that is performed by those with foolish notions, and which involves torturing the self or harming others, is Tamasic.

datavyam iti yad danam diyate 'nupakarine deshe kale cha patre cha tad danam sattvikam smritam

Charity given out of duty, without expectating anything in return, at a proper time and place, and to a worthy person is Satvic.

yat tu pratyupakarartham phalam uddishya va punah diyate cha pariklishtam tad danam rajasam smritam

Charity given expecting something in return or with an intention of some kind of reward, or reluctantly is called Rajasic.

adesha-kale yad danam apatrebhyash cha diyate asat-kritam avajnatam tat tamasam udahritam

Charity given at the wrong place and at the wrong time for an unworthy cause, with a grudge is Tamasic

om tat sad iti nirdesho brahmanas tri-vidhah smritah brahmanas tena vedash cha yajnash cha vihitah pura

"Om Tat Sat" is the symbolic representation of the Supreme Absolute Truth. From which the priests, the scriptures, and the sacrifices came into being at creation.

tasmad om ity udahritya yajna-dana-tapah-kriyah pravartante vidhanoktah satatam brahma-vadinam

Therefore, the chanters of the vedas performing sacrifice, charity and penance in accordance with scriptural regulations always being by uttering Om.

tad ity anabhisandhaya phalam yajna-tapah-kriyah dana-kriyash cha vividhah kriyante moksha-kankshibhih

Who do not expect any rewards, but seek to be free from material entanglements, utter the word "Tat" along with acts of austerity, sacrifice, and charity.

sad-bhave sadhu-bhave cha sad ity etat prayujyate prashaste karmani tatha sach-chhabdah partha yujyate

The Absolute Truth is the objective of devotional sacrifice, and it is indicated by the word 'Sat', O Pritha's son.

yajne tapasi dane cha sthitih sad iti chochyatc karma chaiva tad-arthiyam sad ity evabhidhiyate

When 'Sat' is uttered for Yajna, austerity, or charity it denotes eternal truth and a complete devotion towards Me and that action is performed for My sake.

ashraddhaya hutam dattam tapas taptam kritam cha yat asad ity uchyate partha na cha tat pretya no iha

Any Yajna, charity, austerity, or penance performed without faith in the Supreme, O Pritha's son, is impermanent. It is asat [untrue] and is worthless both in this life and the next.

Chapter 18

arjuna uvacha sannyasasya maha-baho tattvam ichchhami veditum tyagasya cha hrishikesha prithak keshi-nishudana

Arjuna asks: O mighty-armed, I wish to understand the essence and distinction between 'Sannyas' and 'Tyaga', O killer of the Kesi demon, master of the senses.

shri-bhagavan uvacha kamyanam karmanam nyasam sannyasam kavayo viduh sarva-karma-phala-tyagam prahus tyagam vichakshanah

The Lord replies: Renunciation of actions done for rewards is called 'Sannyas' by the knowledgeable, and abandoning the ownership of the results of all actions is called 'Tyaga' by the wise.

tyajyam dosha-vad ity eke karma prahur manishinah yajna-dana-tapah-karma na tyajyam iti chapare

Some scholars believe that all actions are impure and should be renounced. However, some believe that Yajna, charity and austerity should not be renounced.

nishchayam shrinu me tatra tyage bharata-sattama tyago hi purusha-vyaghra tri-vidhah samprakirtitah

My conclusion about 'Tyaga', O scion of Bharat, 'O tiger amongst men, is that there are three types 'Tyaga'.

yajna-dana-tapah-karma na tyajyam karyam eva tat yajno danam tapash chaiva pavanani manishinam

Yajna, charity and austerity should not be renounced, but performed, because these have a purifying effect on the intellect.

etany api tu karmani sangam tyaktva phalani cha kartavyaniti me partha nishchitam matam uttamam

All these [Yajna, charity & austerity] activities should be performed without attachment or any expectation of a reward or ownership. They should be performed as a matter of duty, O Pritha's son, That is My supreme verdict.

niyatasya tu sannyasah karmano nopapadyate mohat tasya parityagas tamasah parikirtitah

Prescribed duties should never be renounced. If one gives up his prescribed duties because of delusion, then such renunciation is says to be Tamasic.

duhkham ity eva yat karma kaya-klesha-bhayat tyajet sa kritva rajasam tyagam naiva tyaga-phalam labhet

Giving up prescribed duties [of Yajna, charity, and austerity] deeming that they are too cumbersome or physically strenuous is 'Tyaga' [renunciation] that is Rajasic. Never benefit from such 'Tyaga'

karyam ity eva yat karma niyatam kriyate 'rjuna sangam tyaktva phalam chaiva sa tyagah sattviko matah

When one performs his prescribed duties [of Yajna, charity, and austerity] as one's responsibility, and renounces the desire of a reward or ownership, O Arjuna, then that 'Tyaga' [renunciation] is says to be Satvic.

na dveshty akushalam karma kushale nanushajjate tyagi sattva-samavishto medhavi chhinna-sanshayah

Who has neither aversion to discomforting nor a preference to a comforting duty is without doubt a established Satvic 'Tyagi'.

na hi deha-bhrita shakyam tyaktum karmany asheshatah yas tu karma-phala-tyagi sa tyagity abhidhiyate

It is indeed impossible for an embodied being to give up all activities. But he who renounces the desire for a reward and the ownership of his actions is a true 'Tyagi'.

anishtam ishtam mishram cha tri-vidham karmanah phalam bhavaty atyaginam pretya na tu sannyasinam kvachit

Desirable, undesireable, or mixed are the three types of rewards & results await the non-'Tyagis' [non-renouncers] after their death, but none for the 'Tyagis'.

panchaitani maha-baho karanani nibodha me sankhye kritante proktani siddhaye sarva-karmanam

Now learn from Me the five factors, O Mighty-armed, that have been mentioned for the accomplishment of all actions in the doctrine of Sankhya.

adhishthanam tatha karta karanam cha prithag-vidham vividhash cha prithak cheshta daivam chaivatra panchamam

The [physical] body, the doer [intellect], sense organs, particular [sense organ's] function and fate being the fifth.

sharira-van-manobhir yat karma prarabhate narah nyayyam va viparitam va panchaite tasya hetavah

Whatever action a body performs, whether just or unjust, either physically, through speech or by thought, these five [body, intellect, sense organs and their individual functions and fate] cause it.

tatraivam sati kartaram atmanam kevalam tu yah pashyaty akrita-buddhitvan na sa pashyati durmatih

Therefore one who thinks himself the only doer, not considering the five factors, is certainly not very intelligent and cannot see things as they are.

yasya nahankrito bhavo buddhir yasya na lipyate hatva 'pi sa imanl lokan na hanti na nibadhyate

Whoever is free from ownership and motive for his actions, even though he may slay living beings, he neither kills nor is he bound by his actions.

jnanam jneyam parijnata tri-vidha karma-chodana karanam karma karteti tri-vidhah karma-sangrahah

Perception, perceived, and perceiver are the three motivators; The senses, the act and the doer are the three constituents of action.

jnanam karma cha karta cha tridhaiva guna-bhedatah prochyate guna-sankhyane yathavach chhrinu tany api

Knowledge, action, and doer, differ according to their inherent Guna [Traits: Satva, Rajas, & Tamas] as described in Sankhya, learn their true nature also.

sarva-bhuteshu yenaikam bhavam avyayam ikshate avibhaktam vibhakteshu taj jnanam viddhi sattvikam

That knowledge by which the indivisible indestructible Supreme One is seen in all living entities, even though they are divided into innumerable forms, that knowledge is Satvic.

prithaktvena tu yaj jnanam nana-bhavan prithag-vidhan vetti sarveshu bhuteshu taj jnanam viddhi rajasam

That knowledge by which one sees that in every different body there is a different type of living entity is Rajasic.

yat tu kritsna-vad ekasmin karye saktam ahaitukam atattvartha-vad alpam cha tat tamasam udahritam

That knowledge which is fixated that there is nothing beyond this physical body, lacking in true insight and petty is Tamasic.

niyatam sanga-rahitam araga-dveshatah kritam aphala-prepsuna karma yat tat sattvikam uchyate

The action which is performed as a duty, without ownership, free from affection or aversion, and without a desire for a reward is Satvic.

yat tu kamepsuna karma sahankarena va punah kriyate bahulayasam tad rajasam udahritam

The action which is performed with great effort by one seeking to gratify his desires, and enacted from a sense of false ego, is Rajasic.

anubandham kshayam hinsam anapekshya cha paurusham mohad arabhyate karma yat tat tamasam uchyate

The action which is performed in delusion, disregarding scriptural injunctions, heedless of its consequences, violent and harmful to others is Tamasic.

mukta-sango 'naham-vadi dhrity-utsaha-samanvitah siddhy-asiddhyor nirvikarah karta sattvika uchyate

The doer who is free from association and ego, filled with courage and enthusiasm, unaffected by success or failure is Satvic.

ragi karma-phala-prepsur lubdho hinsatmako 'shuchih harsha-shokanvitah karta rajasah parikirtitah

The doer who is ambitious, seeks rewards for his actions, greedy, heartless, impure, subject to joy and sorrow, is Rajasic.

ayuktah prakritah stabdhah shatho naishkritiko 'lasah vishadi dirgha-sutri cha karta tamasa uchyate

The doer who is fickle, vulgar, obstinate, deceptive, destructive, insolent, despondent and procrastinating is Tamasic.

buddher bhedam dhritesh chaiva gunatas tri-vidham shrinu prochyamanam asheshena prithaktvena dhananjaya

Now I will tell you in detail about the different kinds of understanding and determination, according to the three traits of nature, O victor of wealth.

pravrittim cha nivrittim cha karyakarye bhayabhaye bandham moksham cha ya vetti buddhih sa partha sattviki

That understanding by which one knows what ought to be done and what ought not to be done, what is to be feared and what is not to be feared, what is binding and what is liberating is Satvic, O Pritha's son.

yaya dharmam adharmam cha karyam chakaryam eva cha ayathavat prajanati buddhih sa partha rajasi

That understanding which cannot distinguish between dharma and adharma, between action and inaction, O Pritha's son, is Rajasic.

adharmam dharmam iti ya manyate tamasavrita sarvarthan viparitansh cha buddhih sa partha tamasi

That understanding which considers adharma to be dharma and vice-versa under the spell of illusion and darkness, and perverts everything, O Pritha's son, is Tamasic.

dhritya yaya dharayate manah-pranendriya-kriyah yogenavyabhicharinya dhritih sa partha sattviki

That determination which is unshakable, which is sustained with steadfastness towards yoga, and which thus controls the activities of the mind, life and senses is Satvic determination, O Pritha's son.

yaya tu dharma-kamarthan dhritya dharayate 'rjuna prasangena phalakankshi dhritih sa partha rajasi

That determination which is held fast by religious activities for a reward, pleasures and wealth, O Arjun, is Rajasic.

yaya svapnam bhayam shokam vishadam madam eva cha na vimunchati durmedha dhritih sa partha tamasi

That determination which does not go beyond dreaming, fearfulness, lamentation, vanity and delusion – such unintelligent determination, O Pritha's son, is Tamasic.

sukham tv idanim tri-vidham shrinu me bharatarshabha abhyasad ramate yatra duhkhantam cha nigachchhati

Now I will describe the three kinds of happiness, O best of Bharats, conditioned by which the Soul revels, ending all sorrows.

yat tad agre visham iva pariname 'mritopamam tat sukham sattvikam proktam atma-buddhi-prasada-jam

That happiness which in the beginning seems like poison but turns out to be like nectar in the end, which awakens self-realization by the mind is Satvic.

vishayendriya-sanyogad yat tad agre 'mritopamam pariname visham iva tat sukham rajasam smritam

That happiness which is derived by the pleasures of senses from the union with their objects and which appears like nectar at first but turns out to be poison at the end is Rajasic.

yad agre chanubandhe cha sukham mohanam atmanah nidralasya-pramadottham tat tamasam udahritam

That happiness which is blind to self-realization, which is delusion from beginning to end and which arises from sleep, laziness and illusion is Tamasic.

na tad asti prithivyam va divi deveshu va punah sattvam prakriti-jair muktam yad ebhih syat tribhir gunaih

Neither on earth nor in the higher realms amongst the demigods or others, is there an entity free from the effect of the three traits of Nature.

brahmana-kshatriya-visham shudranam cha parantapa karmani pravibhaktani svabhava-prabhavair gunaih

Brahmins, Kshatriyas, Vaishyas, and Shudras, O tormentor of foes, is born as per their [previous life's] karmas, as well as separated by the influence of their inherent Gunas [traits]

shamo damas tapah shaucham kshantir arjavam eva cha jnanam vijnanam astikyam brahma-karma svabhava-jam

Peacefulness, self-control, austerity, purity, tolerance, honesty, knowledge, wisdom and piety – these are the indicative attributes of a Brahmin.

shauryam tejo dhritir dakshyam yuddhe chapy apalayanam danam ishvara-bhavash cha kshatram karma svabhava-jam

Valour, strength, fortitude, strategic aptitude, courage in battle, philanthropy and leadership are the indicative attributes of a Kshatriya.

krishi-gau-rakshya-vanijyam vaishya-karma svabhava-jam paricharyatmakam karma shudrasyapi svabhava-jam

Those who are naturally adept at farming, animal husbandry, trading, and commerce are Vaishyas. And those that serve society through their vocational talents are Shudras.

sve sve karmany abhiratah sansiddhim labhate narah sva-karma-niratah siddhim yatha vindati tach chhrinu

Only through dutiful and diligent execution of their respective duties does a being fulfill their destiny and achieves perfection, listen to how its done.

yatah pravrittir bhutanam yena sarvam idam tatam sva-karmana tam abhyarchya siddhim vindati manavah

Who is the source of all beings and who is all-pervading, a man can attain perfection by performing one's role as His worship.

shreyan swa-dharmo vigunah para-dharmat sv-anushthitat svabhava-niyatam karma kurvan napnoti kilbisham

Better to perform one's own role, even if devoid of merit, than well-performing another's role, performing action consonant with one's aptitude man does not incur sin.

saha-jam karma kaunteya sa-dosham api na tyajet sarvarambha hi doshena dhumenagnir ivavritah

An individual might view their duties as vain, O Kunti's son, however, they must not abandon them - for like smoke covers a fire, the true purpose fulfilled by their duties is oft-times hidden from their intellect.

asakta-buddhih sarvatra jitatma vigata-sprihah naishkarmya-siddhim paramam sannyasenadhigachchhati

With mind detached from all yearning through self-realization, a man attains the highest perfection of acting without incurring karmas, by renuniciation.

siddhim prapto yatha brahma tathapnoti nibodha me samasenaiva kaunteya nishtha jnanasya ya para

Having achieved that perfection, listen to how one attains Brahman, I will briefly explain to you, O Kunti's son, that which is the final stage of knowledge.

buddhya vishuddhaya yukto dhrityatmanam niyamya cha shabdadin vishayans tyaktva raga-dveshau vyudasya cha

One becomes fit to attain Brahman when he or she possesses a purified intellect and firmly restrains the senses, abandoning sound and other objects of the senses, casting aside attraction and aversion.

vivikta-sevi laghv-ashi yata-vak-kaya-manasah dhyana-yoga-paro nityam vairagyam samupashritah

Such a person relishes solitude, eats lightly, controls body, mind, and speech, is ever engaged in meditation, and practices dispassion.

ahankaram balam darpam kamam krodham parigraham vimuchya nirmamah shanto brahma-bhuyaya kalpate

Free from egotism, violence, arrogance, desire, possessiveness of property, and selfishness, such a person, situated in tranquility, is fit for union with Brahman [Moksha]

brahma-bhutah prasannatma na shochati na kankshati samah sarveshu bhuteshu mad-bhaktim labhate param

One who is thus transcendentally situated at once realizes the Supreme Brahman and becomes fully joyful. He never laments or desires to have anything. He is equally disposed toward every living entity. In that state he attains pure devotion for Me.

bhaktya mam abhijanati yavan yash chasmi tattvatah tato mam tattvato jnatva vishate tad-anantaram

By devotion one come to know who & what I am in Truth. Then, by knowing My essence, My devotee merges with Me.

sarva-karmany api sada kurvano mad-vyapashrayah mat-prasadad avapnoti shashvatam padam avyayam

Thus My devotees perform all their actions depending on Me, by My grace they attain everlasting and eternal state [Moksha]

chetasa sarva-karmani mayi sannyasya mat-parah buddhi-yogam upashritya mach-chittah satatam bhava

Surrender all actions unto Me mentally, refuged in Yog of the intellect, keep your consciousness immersed in My devotion.

mach-chittah sarva-durgani mat-prasadat tarishyasi atha chet tvam ahankaran na shroshyasi vinankshyasi

By dedicating your devotion to Me, by My grace you shall overcome all obstacles and difficulties. But if, due to pride, you do not listen to My advice, you will perish.

yad ahankaram ashritya na yotsya iti manyase mithyaisha vyavasayas te prakritis tvam niyokshyati

If, motivated by pride, you say, 'You will not fight," your resolve will be futile, because your nature will compel you to fight.

swbhava-jena kaunteya nibaddhah svena karmana kartum nechchhasi yan mohat karishyasy avasho 'pi tat

You may refuse to fight due to delusion, O Kunti's son, but bound by your inherent Karma & qualities of your nature's traits, you will chose fighting.

ishvarah sarva-bhutanam hrid-deshe 'rjuna tishthati bhramayan sarva-bhutani yantrarudhani mayaya

The Supreme Lord is situated in everyone's heart, O Arjuna, but Maya [illusion formed by their traits of Nature] drives them, like a driver driving a vehicle.

tam eva sharanam gachchha sarva-bhavena bharata tat-prasadat param shantim sthanam prapsyasi shashvatam

O scion of scion of Bharat, surrender unto Him completely. By His grace you will attain transcendental peace and the supreme and eternal abode.

iti te jnanam akhyatam guhyad guhyataram maya vimrishyaitad asheshena yathechchhasi tatha kuru

Thus I have explained to you the profoundest of confidential knowledge. Deliberate over it deeply, and then do as you wish.

sarva-guhyatamam bhuyah shrinu me paramam vachah ishto 'si me dridham iti tato vakshyami te hitam

Listen to My most confidential supreme words, because you are My dear friend and they are for your benefit.

man-mana bhava mad-bhakto mad-yaji mam namaskuru mam evaishyasi satyam te pratijane priyo 'si me

Always think of Me, be devoted to Me, worship Me, and offer obeisance to Me. Doing so, you will certainly come to Me. This is My pledge to you, for you are very dear to Me.

sarva-dharman parityajya mam ekam sharanam vraja aham tvam sarva-papebhyo mokshayishyami ma shuchah

Give up every other activity and simply surrender unto Me alone. I shall liberate you from all sins; do not worry.

idam te natapaskyaya nabhaktaya kadachana na chashushrushave vachyam na cha mam yo 'bhyasutayi

This confidential knowledge may never be explained to those who are not austere, or devoted, or engaged in devotional service, nor to one who is envious of Me.

ya idam paramam guhyam mad-bhakteshv abhidhasyati bhaktim mayi param kritva mam evaishyaty asanshayah

Whosoever interprets and teaches this most profound doctrine to My devotees with supreme devotion in Me, will come to Me.

na cha tasman manushyeshu kashchin me priya-krittamah bhavita na cha me tasmad anyah priyataro bhuvi

There none is more dearer to Me then him [the interpreter & teacher] amongst men, neither will there ever be anyone else more dearer on earth than him.

adhyeshyate cha ya imam dharmyam samvadam avayoh jnana-yajnena tenaham ishtah syam iti me matih

And whosoever studies this sacred dialogue of ours, will be worshipping Me through Yajna of knowledge, this is My opinion.

shraddhavan anasuyash cha shrinuyad api yo narah so 'pi muktah shubhanl lokan prapnuyat punya-karmanam

Whosoever listens to this [profound knowledge] whole heartedly and without ill feelings, after death will attain the blessed pious realms of the righteous.

kachchid etach chhrutam partha tvayaikagrena chetasa kachchid ajnana-sammohah pranashtas te dhananjaya

Did you listen, O Pritha's son, with an attentive mind, is your delusion of ignorance been destroyed, O victor of wealth?

arjuna uvacha nashto mohah smritir labdha tvat-prasadan mayachyuta sthito 'smi gata-sandehah karishye vachanam tava

Arjun replies - Destroyed is my delusion and I have regained my senses by Thy grace, O Unwavering. There are no doubts left and I shall do Thy bidding.

sanjaya uvacha ity aham vasudevasya parthasya cha mahatmanah samvadam imam ashrausham adbhutam roma-harshanam

Sanjay says - Thus have I heard the conversation of two great souls, Krishna and Arjun. And so wonderful is that message that my hair are standing on end.

vyasa-prasadach chhrutavan etad guhyam aham param yogam yogeshvarat krishnat sakshat kathayatah svayam

[Sanjay says] By the mercy of Vyasa, I have heard these most confidential dialogue between the master of all mysticism, Krishna, who was speaking personally to Arjun.

rajan sansmritya sansmritya samvadam imam adbhutam keshavarjunayoh punyam hrishyami cha muhur muhuh

[Sanjay says] O King, as I repeatedly recall this wondrous and holy dialogue between Krishna and Arjun, I take pleasure, being thrilled at every moment.

tach cha sansmritya sansmritya rupam aty-adbhutam hareh vismayo ye mahan rajan hrishyami cha punah punah

[Sanjay says] O King, as I remember the wonderful form of Lord Krishna, I am struck with wonder more and more, and I rejoice again and again.

yatra yogeshvarah krishno yatra partho dhanur-dharah tatra shrir vijayo bhutir dhruva nitir matir mama

[Sanjay says] Wherever there is Krishna, the master of all mystics, and wherever there is Arjun, the supreme archer, there will also certainly be opulence, victory, extraordinary power, and morality. That is my opinion.

| Om Tat Sat | Om Tat Sat | Om Tat Sat |

Also by Shri Vande Bharti

Shri Suktam Havan Vidhi
Timeless Wisdom for Modern Life: The Shrimad Bhagavad Gita

Watch for more at https://www.vandeshri.com.

9 798227 432803